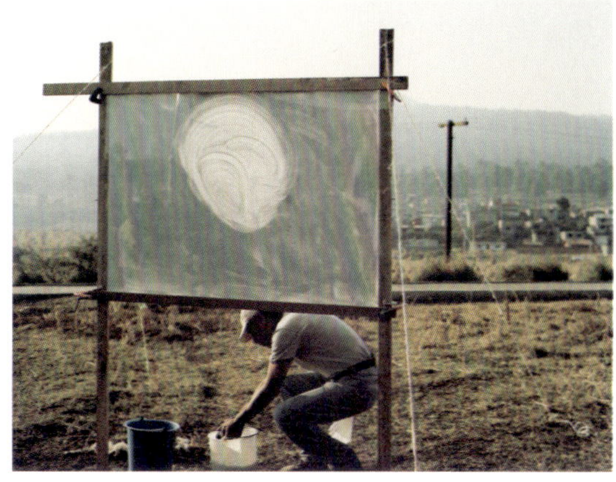

For Francisco, Victor and Yolanda

Color print from process of filming *Parres III*, 2005

Melanie Smith Parres

A&R Press/Turner, Galería OMR and Galerie Peter Kilchmann

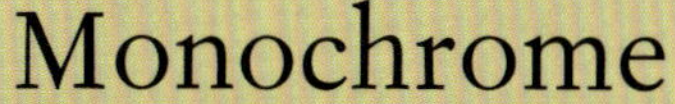

Monochrome

probably always begins with absence.
Absence is harder to define. - except
by an impression left behind. So where
does the work begin or end?

The Question about the beginning of the
end - and about still possibility of
painting.
The beginning of the end being our history.

→ modernism (?)

Extract from notebook, 2006

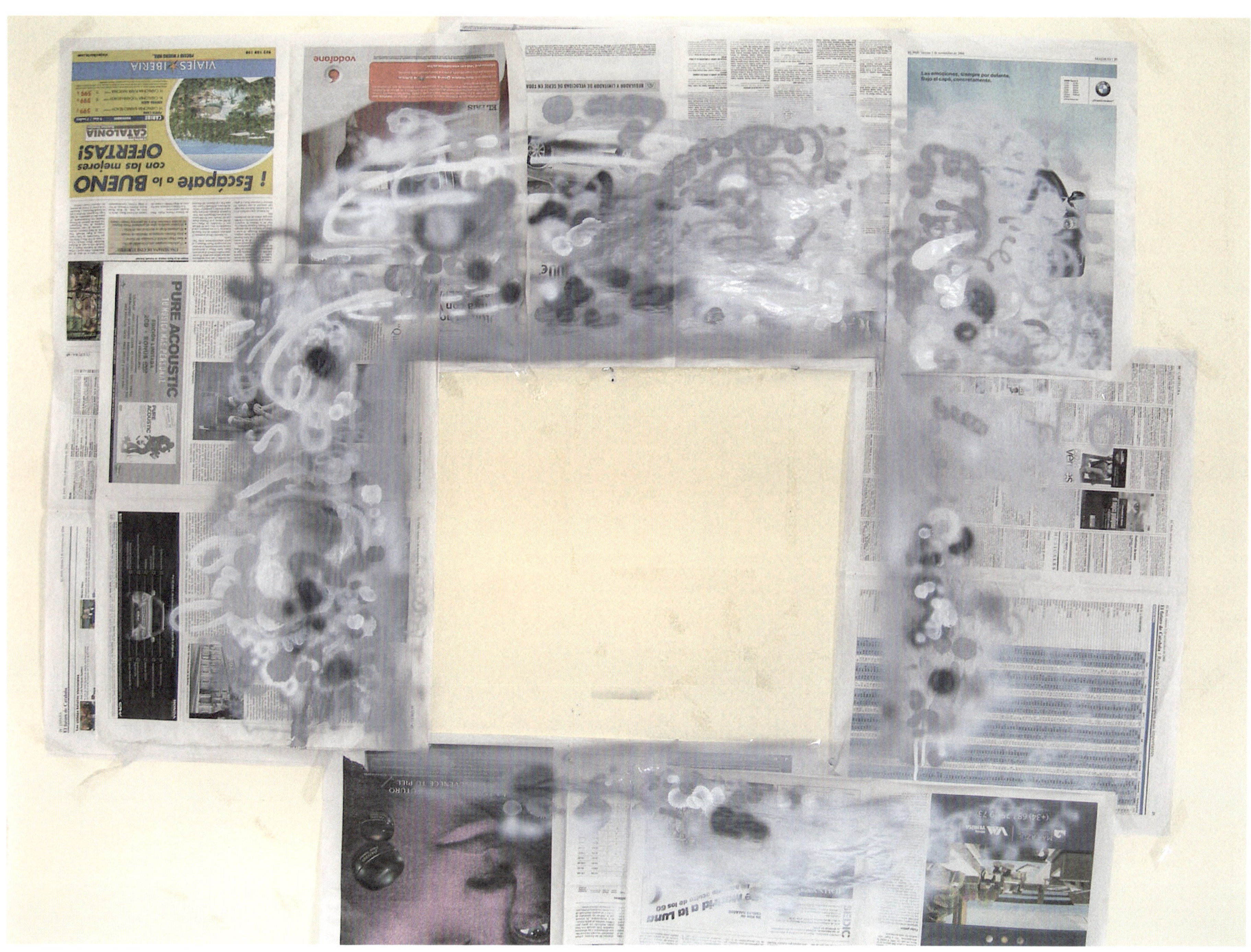

Painting marks left by the process of making a painting in the studio, 2006. 85 × 100 cm

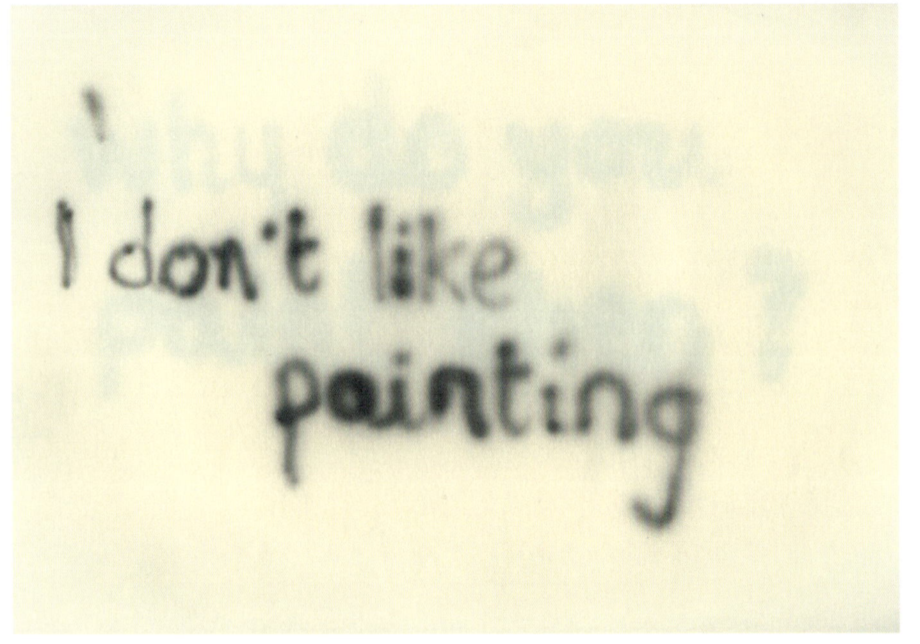
I don't like
painting

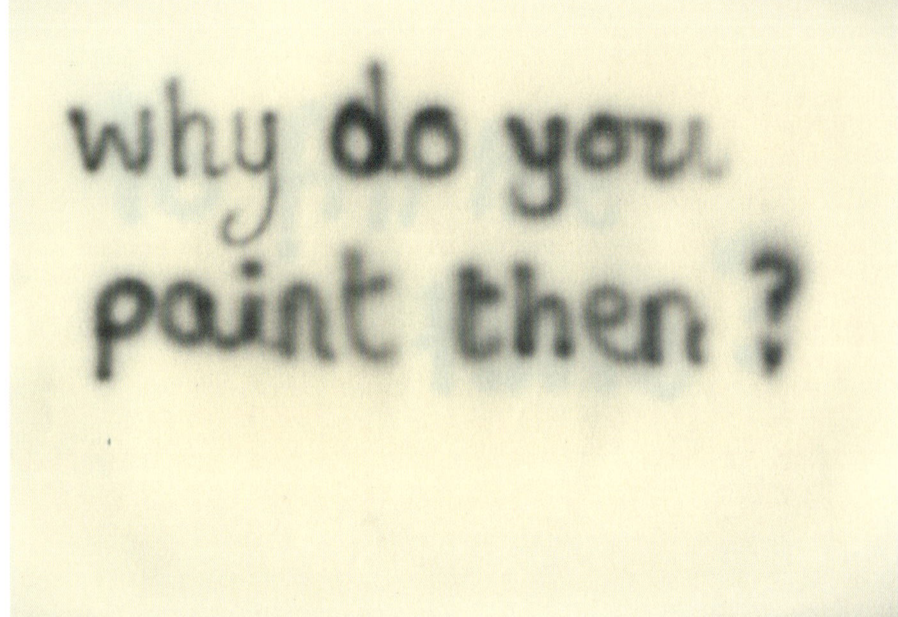
why do you
paint then ?

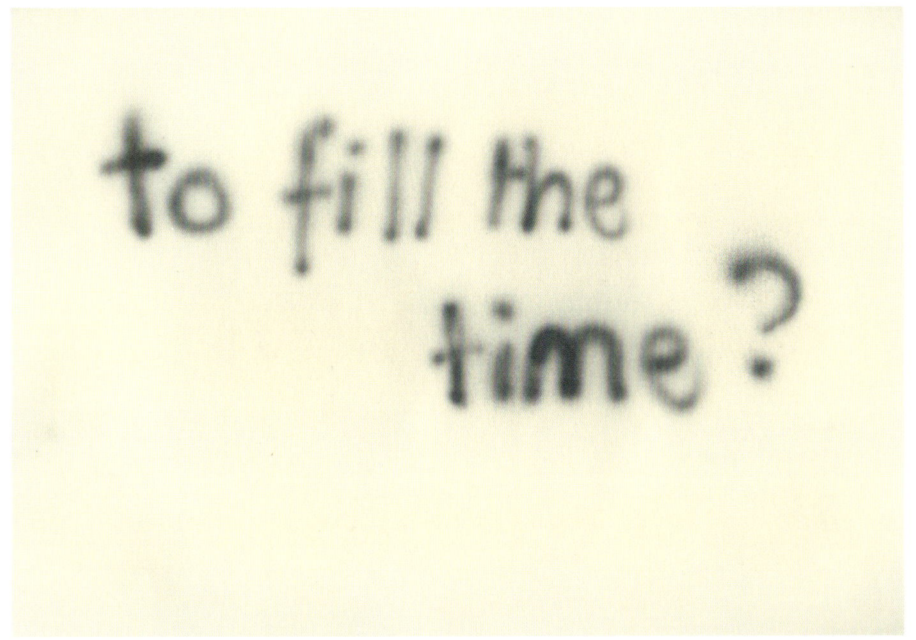

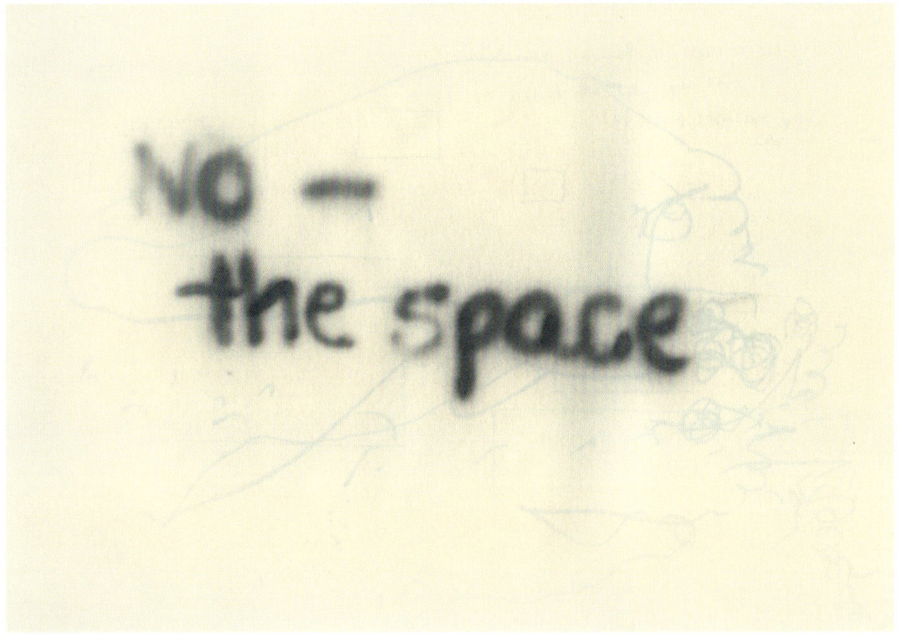

Extract from notebook, 2006

Negative paintings are like a kind of signature – the witness to the painting. The witness that something has been made. We are confronted with the time during the process of the making of the painting (a painting without a painting) – of wasted time. But it's all wasted time. Maybe during the process of the non painting the artist stared at the blank space of the wall, wondering if she should fill a blank space with another blank space. But nowadays there are too many blank spaces – the blank space needs to be filled with the real space (or is it the other way round?) Or the real spaces are too real, and the blanks too blank. Anyway the question won't go away. A painting without illusion…a painting that brings us back to the front of the unpainted canvas.

Melanie Smith

A piece of Monochrome.

With the first totters.
Bandied back and forth.
To now.
Up at nightfall. every nightfall.
No such thing as none.
Was standing. When last went out.
Blank wall.
So stands there facing blank wall.
Ever less, Like light at nightfall.
Blank pinpocked surface, once white in shadow.
Stands there facing the wall staring beyond.
Nothing there either, Nothing stirring anywhere.
Foot of pallet just visible edge of frame.
Then slow fade up of a faint form.
Starless moonless heaven. Dies on to dawn
and never dies.
Window gone

"A Piece of Monochrome"
as written by Samuel Beckett

See the

Window appears in frame.
Frame disguised by window.
But window to clear blank surface.
Bandied back and forth – not sure of it's position.
Totally out of context. ⟶ from beginning to end.
Here there's no such thing as none.
Ever less, like light at nightfall.
Blank pinpocked surface. once white in shadow.
Pedals on staring beyond. Nothing there either
in the landscape. No such landscape.
First step to "transformation" ⟶ (wrong word).
Dusty, abandoned landscape.
First step to somewhere else.
Nothing there either, nothing stirring anywhere.
Painful, working landscape.
Dying to get away – but dies on to dawn

"A Piece of Monochrome"
as written by Melanie Smith

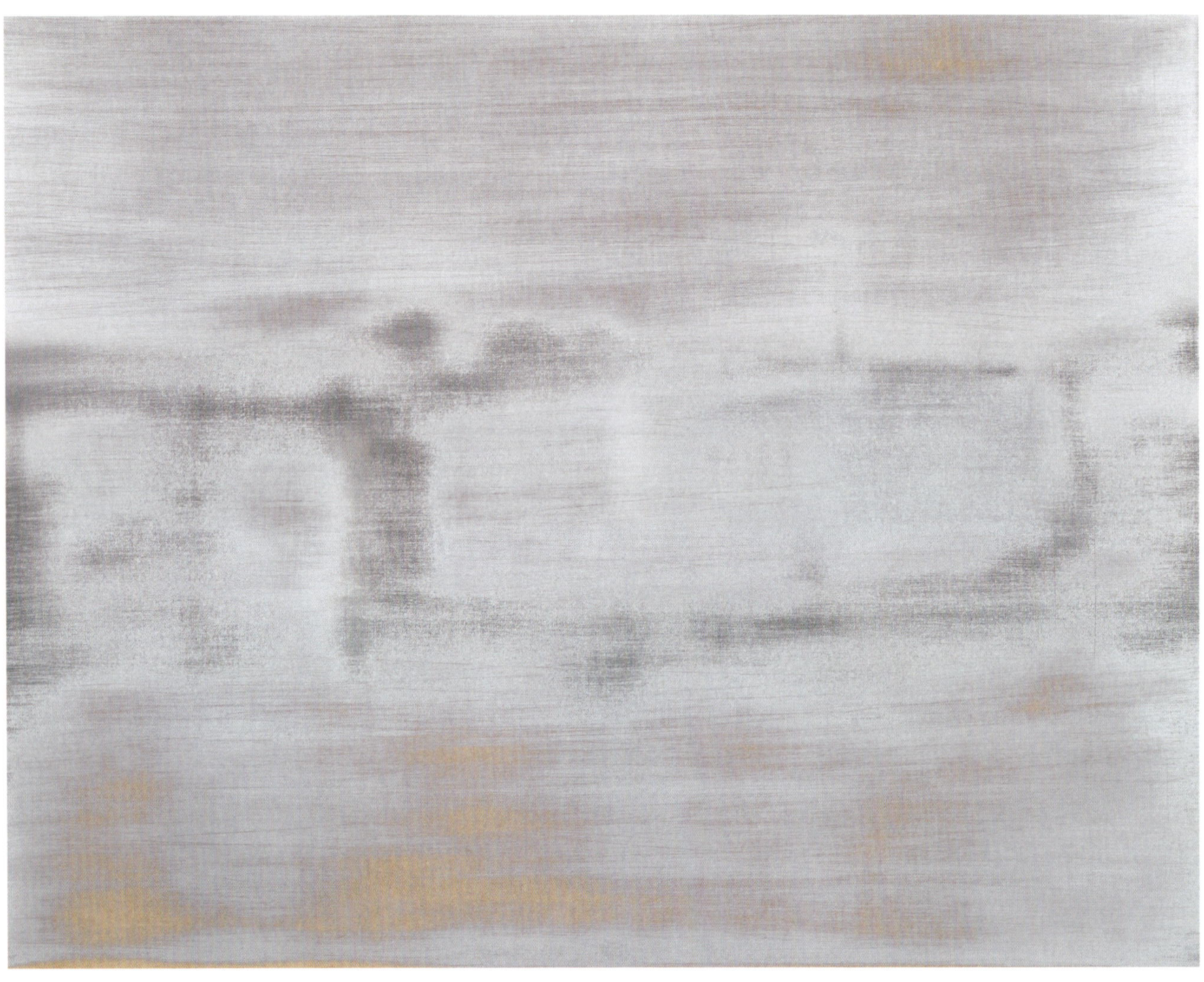

Parres (small series of 4 paintings. No. 1), 2005. 40 × 50 cm

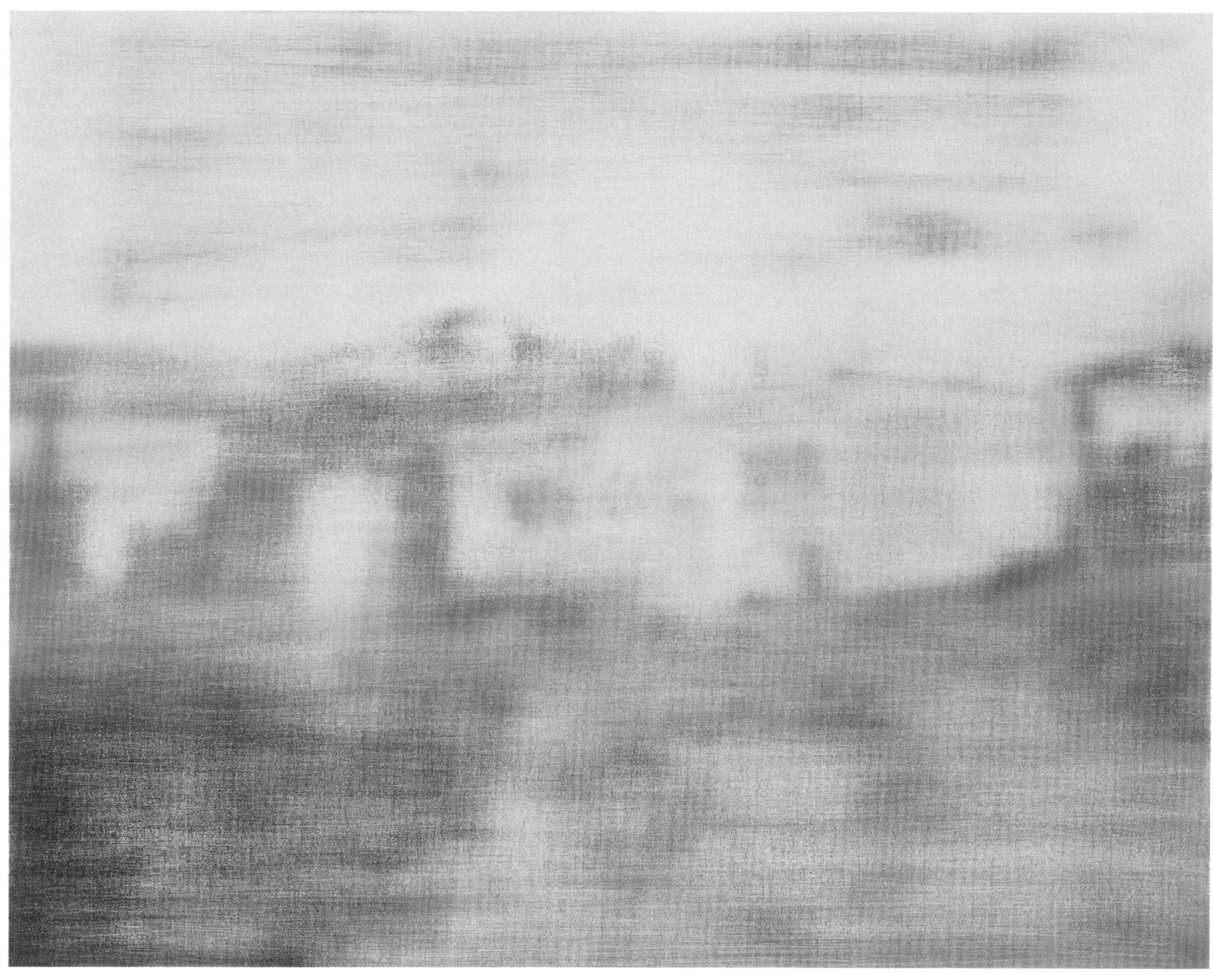

Parres (small series of 4 paintings. No. 2), 2005. 40 × 50 cm

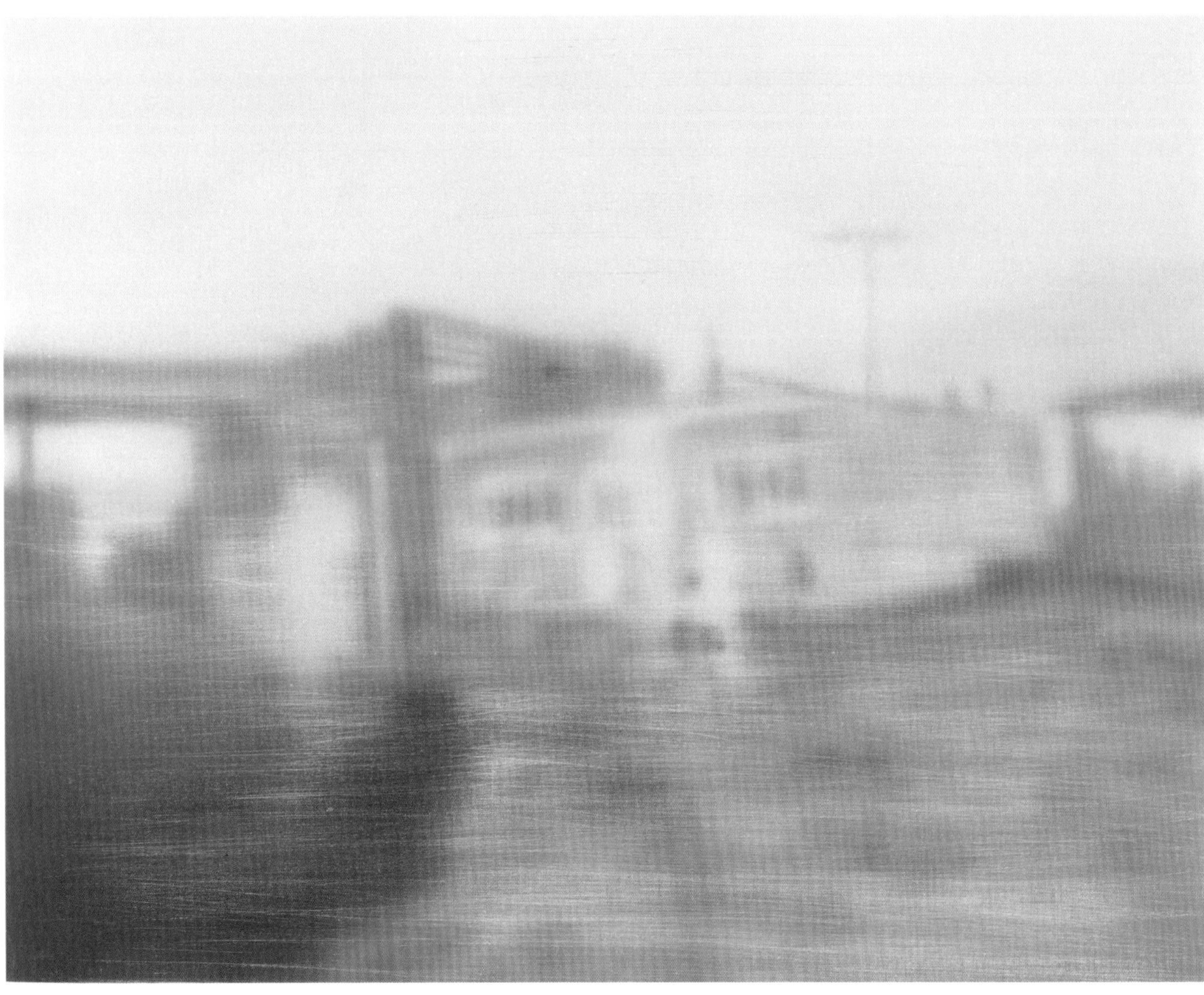

Parres (small series of 4 paintings. No. 3), 2005. 40 × 50 cm

Parres (small series of 4 paintings. No. 4), 2005. 40 × 50 cm

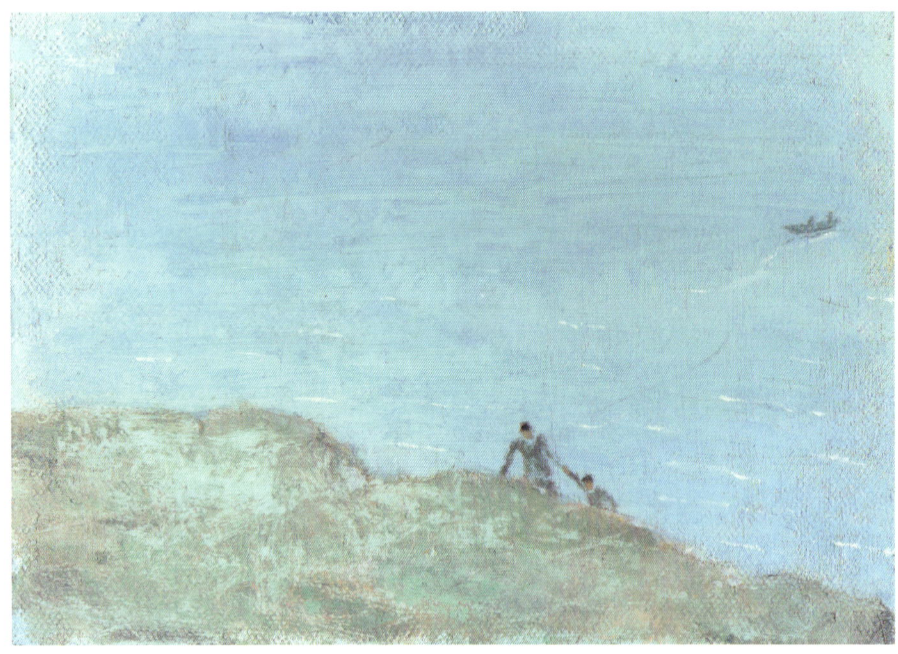

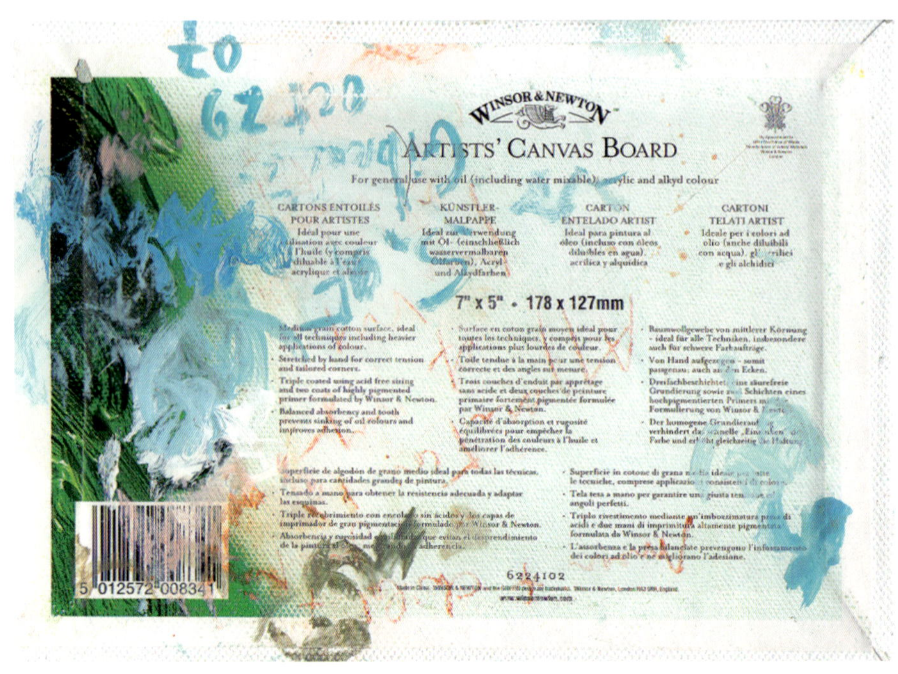

Francis Alÿs, *Untitled* (Strait of Gibraltar), 2007. Oil on canvas, 12.7 × 17.8 cm

Last year I had an accident. I lost the ability to finish a painting. I paint images. Situations that can only exist on a canvas. Now the not finished images get covered by other not finished images that will in turn get lost. The only thing I have been able to finish were a few "real" images. By "real" I mean that they copy reality. Small landscapes or cityscapes that I do when I travel. They are easy to finish because they don't require any invention or projection. They are totally in the present. I am just sitting in front of a scene, outside of it but completely immersed in my perception of it. No: completely immersed in the perception of my self in front of it. My own, yes, but much more the perception of my presence by those people who belong to the scene I am painting. What do they see? The recto of my canvas at first, and if they pass me and look over my shoulder, they see what they could not see a second ago (as they were still walking in the scene I was painting).

And what do I find when I look at these paintings later on? The exact memory of how I was then, on the verso side of the canvas looking at those people, there, on the recto side, with this thin painted cardboard in between us.

Francis Alÿs

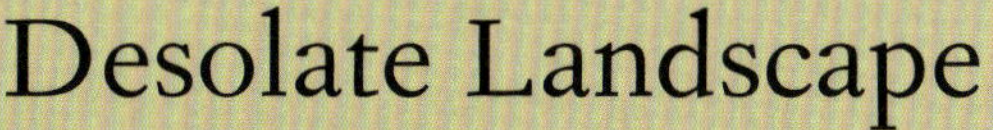
Desolate Landscape

For me the word *pueblo*[1] has always been a synonym of Nahuátzen, my father's birthplace in the mountainous P'urhépecha region of Michoacán. I visited the pueblo at least twice a year until my grandmother, Helena Villegas Paleo, died in the first week of March 2001. Going to the pueblo meant saying hello to everyone on the street, going to the square to exchange used magazines, visiting relatives, eating amazing food and spending hours and hours chatting with people who went to see my grandmother: they came in without knocking and when they were in the inner courtyard they intoned a sort of greeting that included a long, high-pitched "Aunt Helenaaaaaaaaaaaaaaaaaaaaaaa," which my grandmother answered with curses, celebrating the cavalier intrusion of her happy-go-lucky visitors. At some point I found out that the word *p'urhépecha* in the P'urhépecha language meant "those who visit each other," and in the pueblo *everybody* visits everybody else, always taking along some sort of gift, however modest. *Everybody* also leaves with a gift: nuts, an apple, bread or a piece of cheese. We chatted around the fire – the hearth my grandmother had in the middle of her kitchen, a room whose incredibly low ceiling was completely blackened with soot. But people also chat, standing, when they run into each other on the street or in the stores, buying and selling. Everybody knows everybody and is used to the fact that *everybody* also knows everything about *everybodyelse*. *Everybody* helps everybody else if need be, and everybody hates someone who doesn't help out, who stirs up trouble, who speaks on others' behalf in his or her own interest.

And yet, those who speak on behalf of the pueblo have been governing it for many years and keep doing as they please, taking advantage of people's good faith and gullibility. There have always been certain types who, giving almost nothing in return, make use of people's energy, of their spontaneous solidarity, to "bring grist to their own mill": they speak for *everybody*, for the pueblo. Decades have gone by and the pueblo has been almost entirely deserted by the younger folk, who cross over into the United States illegally to earn money and send it back to their families, sometimes in order to take them back to the States with them in search of a better life. The money they send from up north, the so-called "remittances," represents the second largest source of income not only for Nahuátzen but for Mexico as a whole. People occasionally return to the pueblo to see their families on the day of the town's patron saint (in Nahuátzen, it's Saint Louis King of France), on Christmas and on New Year's, and then venture on the long and risky road back to their jobs in the U.S. In the pueblo's name, many politicians have gotten rich and given nothing to those they so eagerly defend – nothing but depression, poverty, misery. Before people started leaving the countryside to go to the U.S., they used go to big cities, like Mexico City, where they had to overcome the most deplorable circumstances and twists of fate, sometimes worse than what had made them leave their homes, their people, their pueblo.

Gildardo "El Güero" Prado, my dad's cousin, left Nahuátzen and went to Mexico City in the 1960s; he got a job in construction, and illegally occupied a plot of land in what was then the south end of the city, where other people from Nahuátzen had done the same. It was on uneven, rocky ground riddled with ravines and caves of volcanic stone – the solidified lava flows left by an eruption of the Xitle volcano thousands of years ago. A surly ethnic group, the Cuicuilcas, had once lived there, ruling over the region; they had even built a circular pyramid, like those called *yácatas* made by the P'urhépechas in Michoacán. Just as the eruption had forced the Cuicuilcas to leave the lava fields, misery had brought El Güero to the lava fields of the capital. Some of El Güero's brothers and in-laws – and even his parents, Aunt Tachi and Uncle Vicente, who opened a *tortillería* – followed him to the neighborhood, which had then been named the Colonia Ajusco, because of the nearby Ajusco mountain that overlooks its craggy landscape. My dad arrived there with his cousin Miguel Avilés, who was a musician and a schoolteacher and who had already tried his luck in the US. My uncle Miguel finally went back to the pueblo, where he ended up teaching music, forming a band – *Los Cheevo's*, which played any kind of music you requested – as well as organizing the town band and opening a poultry shop; my dad stayed, and, like El Güero and many other fellow townspeople, he built what would one day become his home. He built it little by little, depending on the money he had available, without a pre-set budget, or plans, or an architect, or basic services like running water, electricity. or sewerage. Collaboration between neighbors was an everyday thing – to help someone who had managed to set aside enough money to build an extra bedroom for a daughter who had grown up, to set up storefront that would become a convenience store or a car repair shop, to put a roof up or install electricity; *everybody* pitched in. Naturally, these collective activities were accompanied by music, drinks, a party. Some people began to organize themselves to obtain legal property rights to the land they had occupied in an area where more people would soon settle, with or without means, and even further out beyond where they were. In those fledgling neighborhood organizations' demonstrations, *everybody* joined in singing, "*El pueblo, unido, jamás sera vencido…*" (The people, united, will never be defeated), "*El pueblo uniformado, también es explotado…*" (The people in uniform are also exploited)[2] and other slogans they appropriated from opposition political parties and other causes and struggles that had also faced official repression.

The houses that have been built since then in my neighborhood have conserved their "definitely unfinished" status to this day, to the extent that needs, population, means, and customs have changed and continue to change. What they call a *favela* in other countries and a "lost city" here – not to mention nomenclatures that refer to it as "vernacular architecture," that is to say, as an expression of the pueblo – occurs in different places around the world as a concrete manifestation of an urgent need, of the capacity to improvise with the resources at hand, without demagogy, without kitsch. The urban chaos, the lack of planning, the corruption, the disorder, and the accelerated growth of illegal settlements on a much bigger scale – like the exemplary Ciudad Nezahualcóyotl – implies a way of building that transcends aesthetics, that blends visually into an organic and solidary whole, in which people contribute human capital to one another's needs, extending private space into the streets, with improvised soccer games and the sharing of basic chores. I don't know if this is the case for *everybody*, but to me, in terms of my process, in the house where I was born and raised, all of this is also a synonym of the word pueblo.

Abraham Cruzvillegas

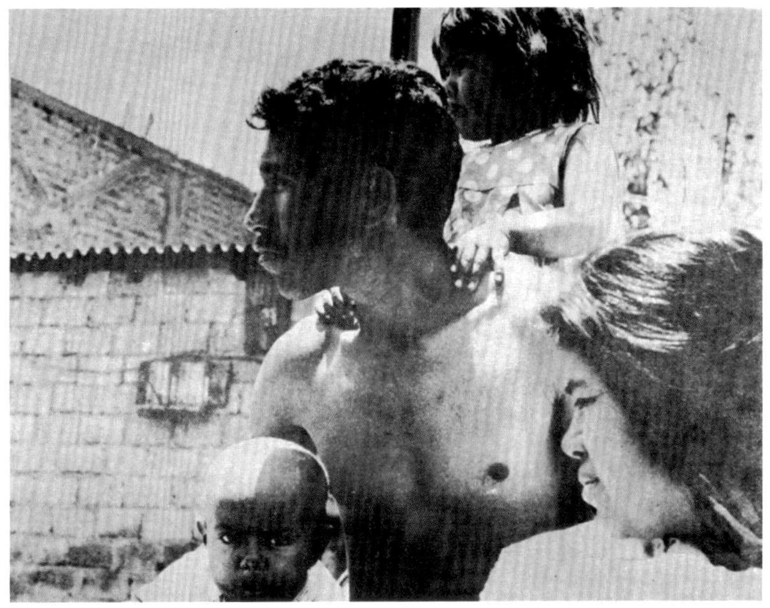

Gildardo "El Güero" Prado

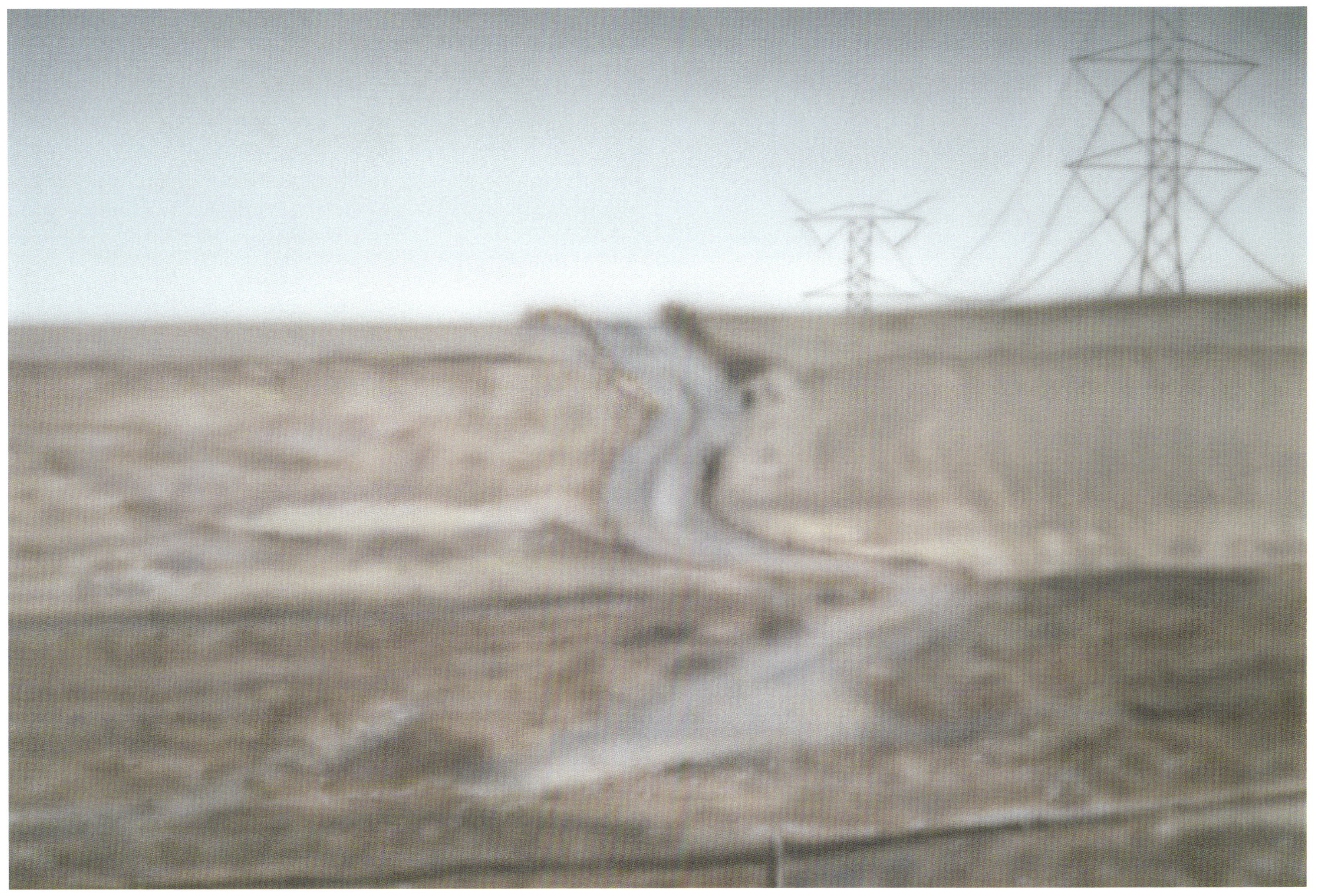

Parres 12, 2007. Acrylic enamel on acrylic, 90 × 135 cm

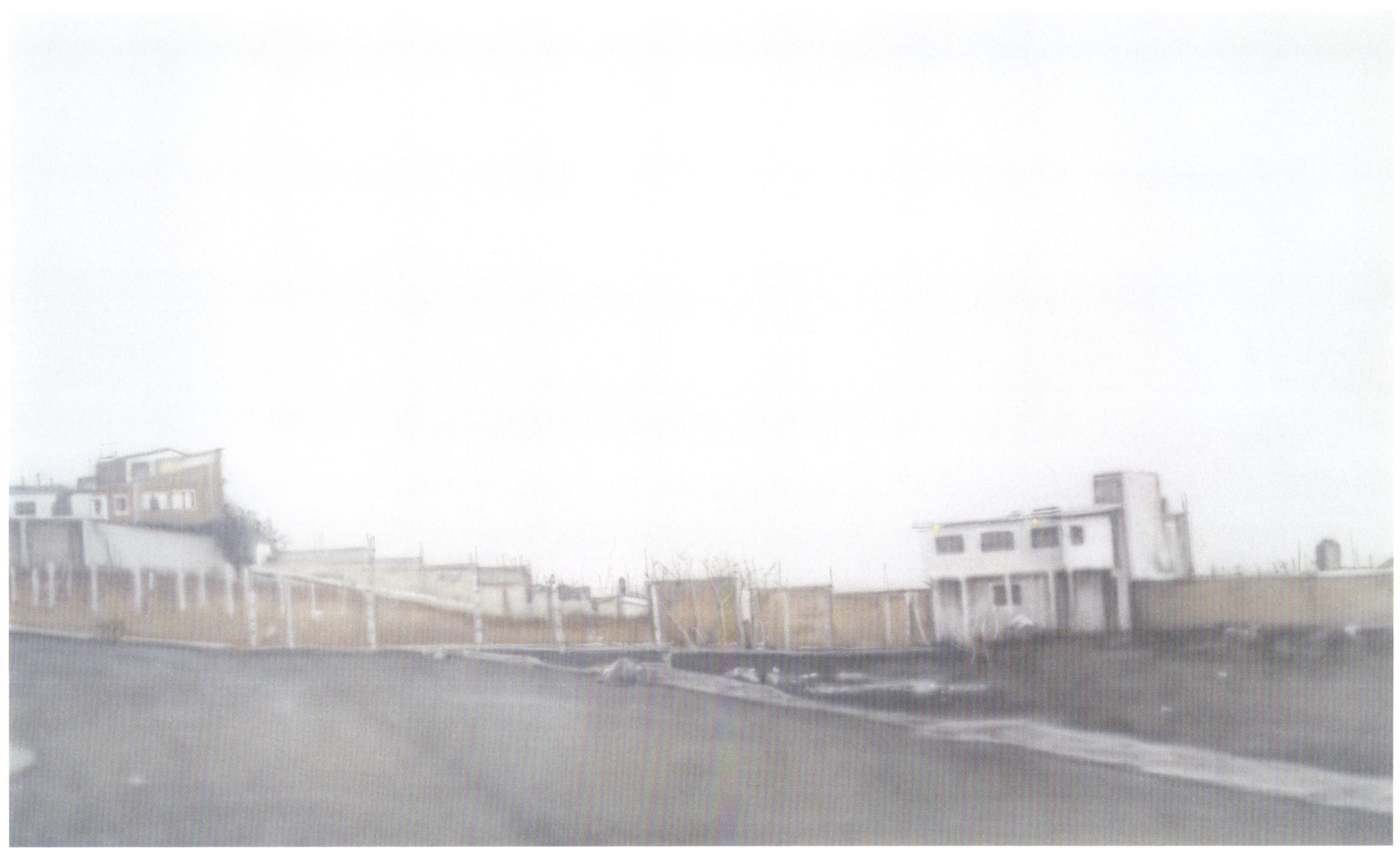

Parres 9, 2006. Acrylic enamel on acrylic, 130 × 200 cm

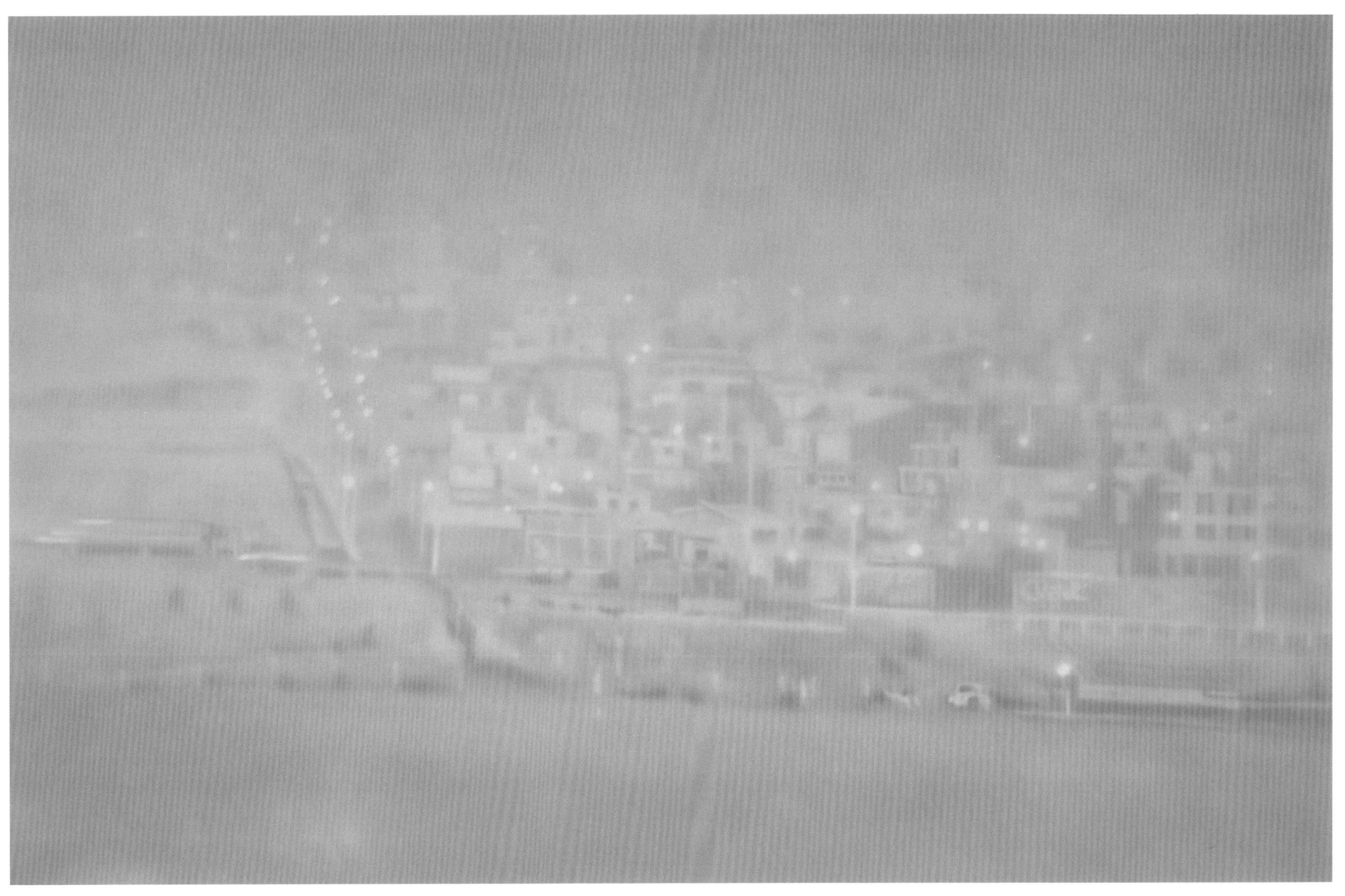

Parres 10, 2006–7. Acrylic enamel on acrylic, 130 × 200 cm

Parres 10, from 2006, is a single, autonomous work in two dimensions, acrylic paint applied onto a smooth acrylic surface. As a representation, the painting depicts a sloping hillside of the town of Parres, covered with houses that are built close to one another. The viewer can recognize the square windows, angled roofs and horizontal walls of these small dwellings. Glowing, vertical lampposts line a narrow street that moves up the center of this view. Running across the bottom of the painting appears to be a dirt field, in which a white car is represented on the right side. Nearby, a wall covered by graffiti is visible. All of these details are seen through what would appear to be a dense fog or cloud, which modulates the clarity of these elements within the frame of the painting. Visibility is concentrated within the center and moves toward greater obscurity at the edges of the work. This misty view, combined with the subtle range of colors in the painting – a play of lavenders, tans, peaches and pinks – give the impression that we are looking at an image of Parres at dawn or dusk. This temporal evocation and its specific palette give the image a romantic tone, a sense of mystery or magic; references that seem far from the reality of Parres as an economically poor town, made up of roughly constructed, gray concrete buildings.

As an abstraction, the painting presents three horizontal bands, which in tone fade into one another, a monochromatic band of brown-tan at the bottom and a purple-lavender band at the top, separated by a central horizon made up of a loose patterning of horizontal squares and planes of gray-purples and narrow vertical lines of peach-pinks. This central area includes other horizontal pink lines, almost white, as well as circular spots of light peach-pinks, both of which are the lightest chromatic elements in the composition. Due to the airbrush painting technique engaged by the artist, these geometric elements, while distinctly present, never appear in sharp outline and evade evidence of manual gesture. These shapes maintain a muted quality as tonal elements within the overall, deceptively monochromatic character of the painting.

Parres 10 offers an unusual planar shift, through which its representational qualities and abstract characteristics come to challenge one another. The angle of the represented image of the town of Parres plays a crucial role in this complex pictorial play. In a previous series of paintings, *Spiral City*, Smith presented views of Mexico City based on photos taken of the city grid from high above it. In many of these works, the view of looking directly down upon the city stressed the flatness of the representation, a quality that the artist took advantage of in creating painterly abstractions of the city that directly referenced the flatness of the plane of the painting surface. In these previous works the plane of the city grid and the plane of the painted surface were spatially unified or were presented as equivalents. With the particular angle of the view of the hillside in *Parres 10*, this unity is broken. The spatial representation in the image here implies a depth; moving from the brown field at the bottom, this site is viewed as shifting back, the town moving upward at an angle that is moving away from both the viewer and the picture plane. While the relationships between the representational forms of the walls, roofs and lights convey this spatial articulation, they continue to maintain their character as abstract painterly forms layered onto the painting surface. These elements thus look to be alternatively read as purely abstract. As such, they appear to separate themselves from their role as representational-signifying elements and float toward the surface of the painting, thereby contradicting the depth that their role as representations imply. This discrepancy creates an interstice, between the implied space of the representation and the physical space of the painted abstraction. It is in its unique articulation of this spatial-optical gap that the strength of this painting lies and here that its crucial role in the continued development of the artist´s dialectical investigations between representation and abstraction in painting is revealed.

Tobias Ostrander

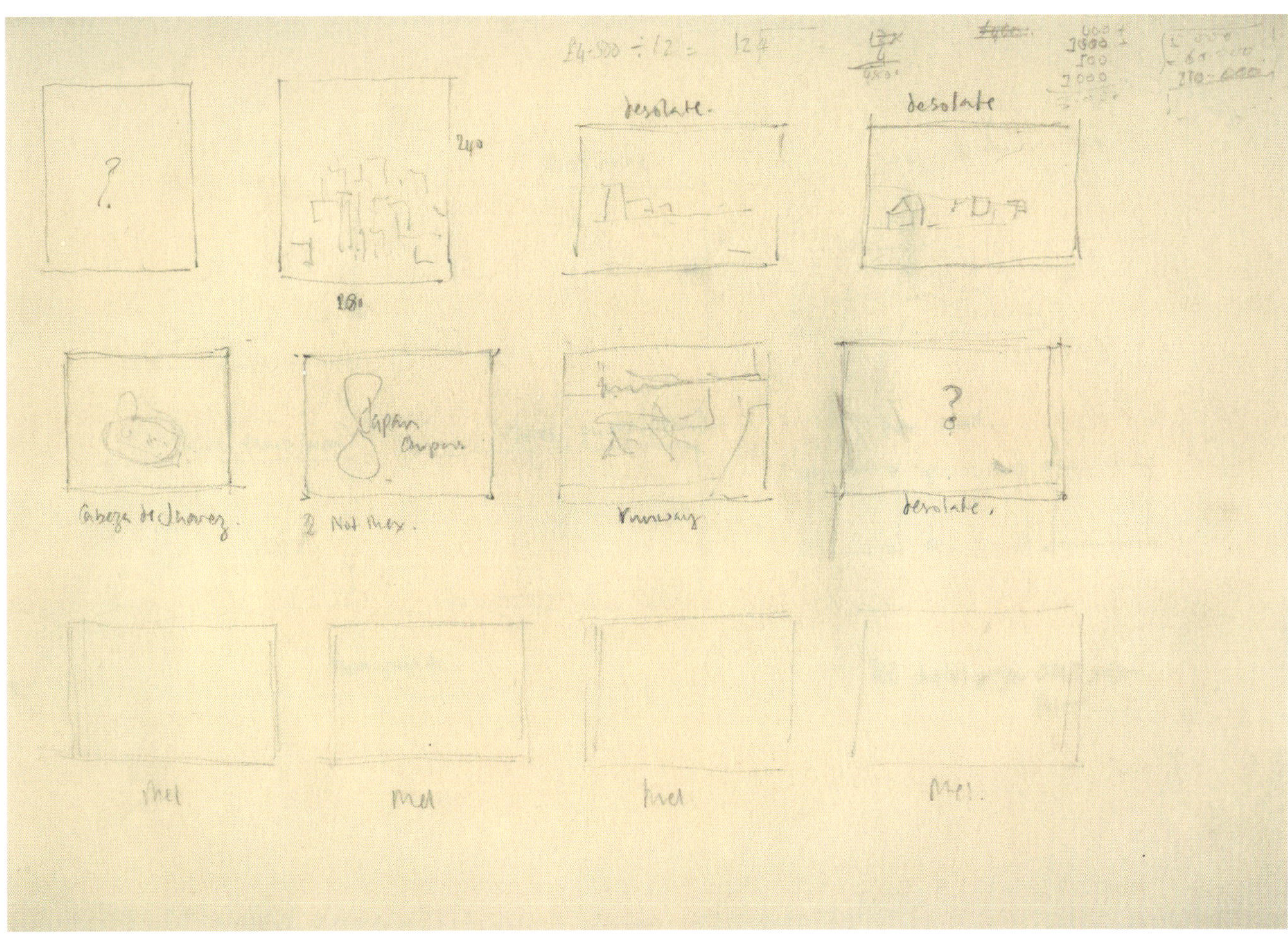

Extract from notebook, 2006

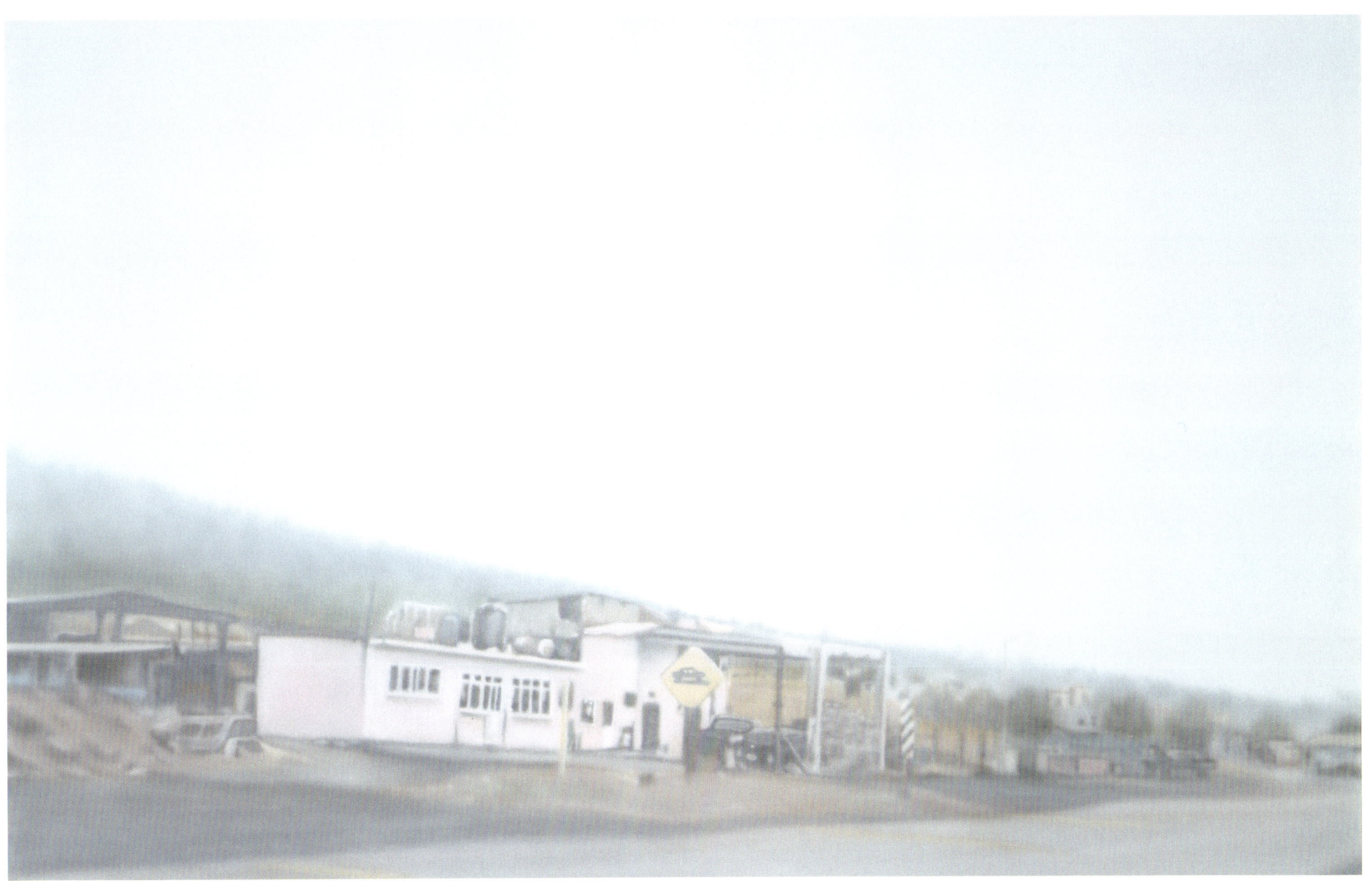

Parres 7, 2006. Acrylic enamel on acrylic, 130 × 200 cm

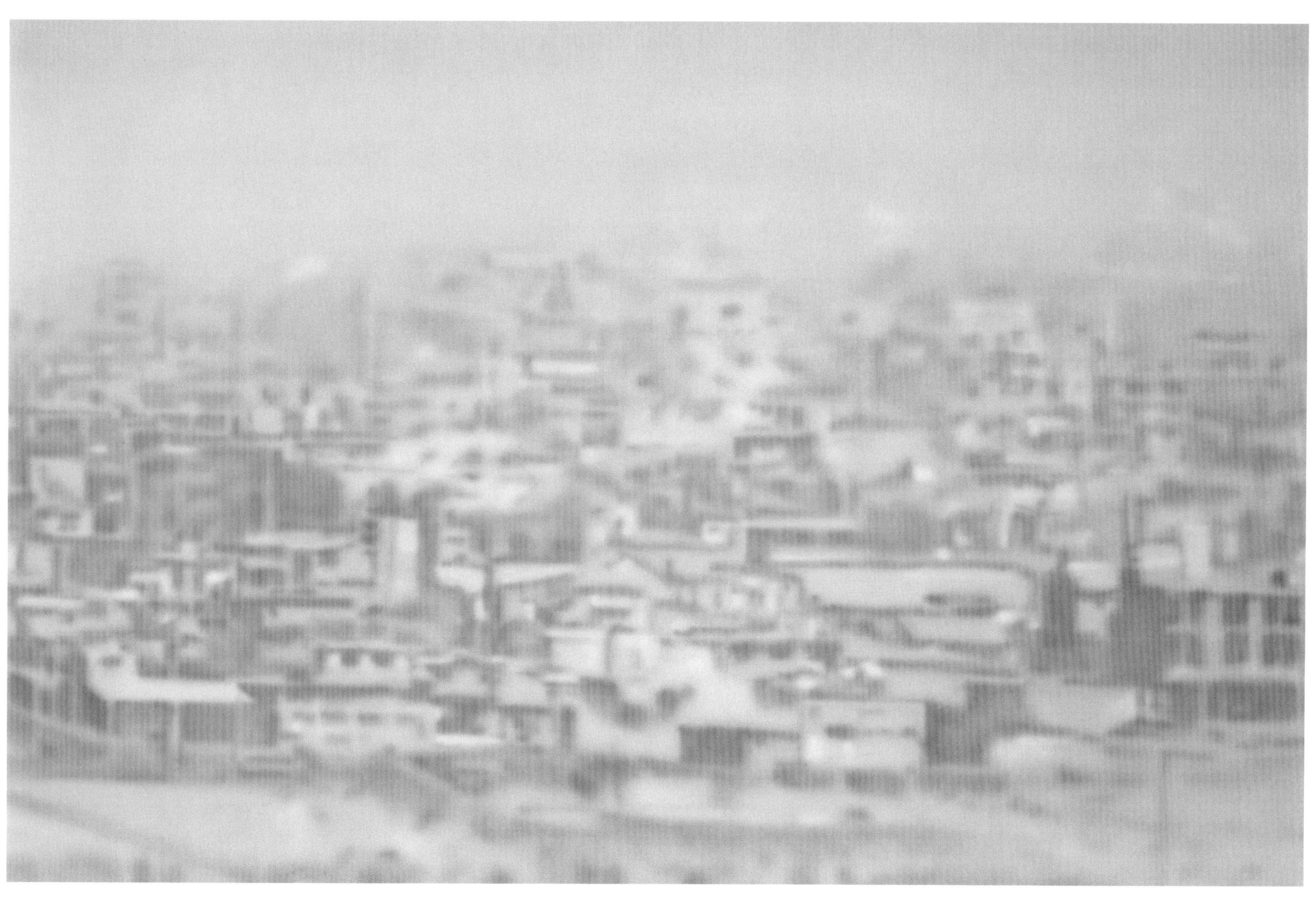

Parres 13, 2007. Acrylic enamel on acrylic, 115 × 175 cm

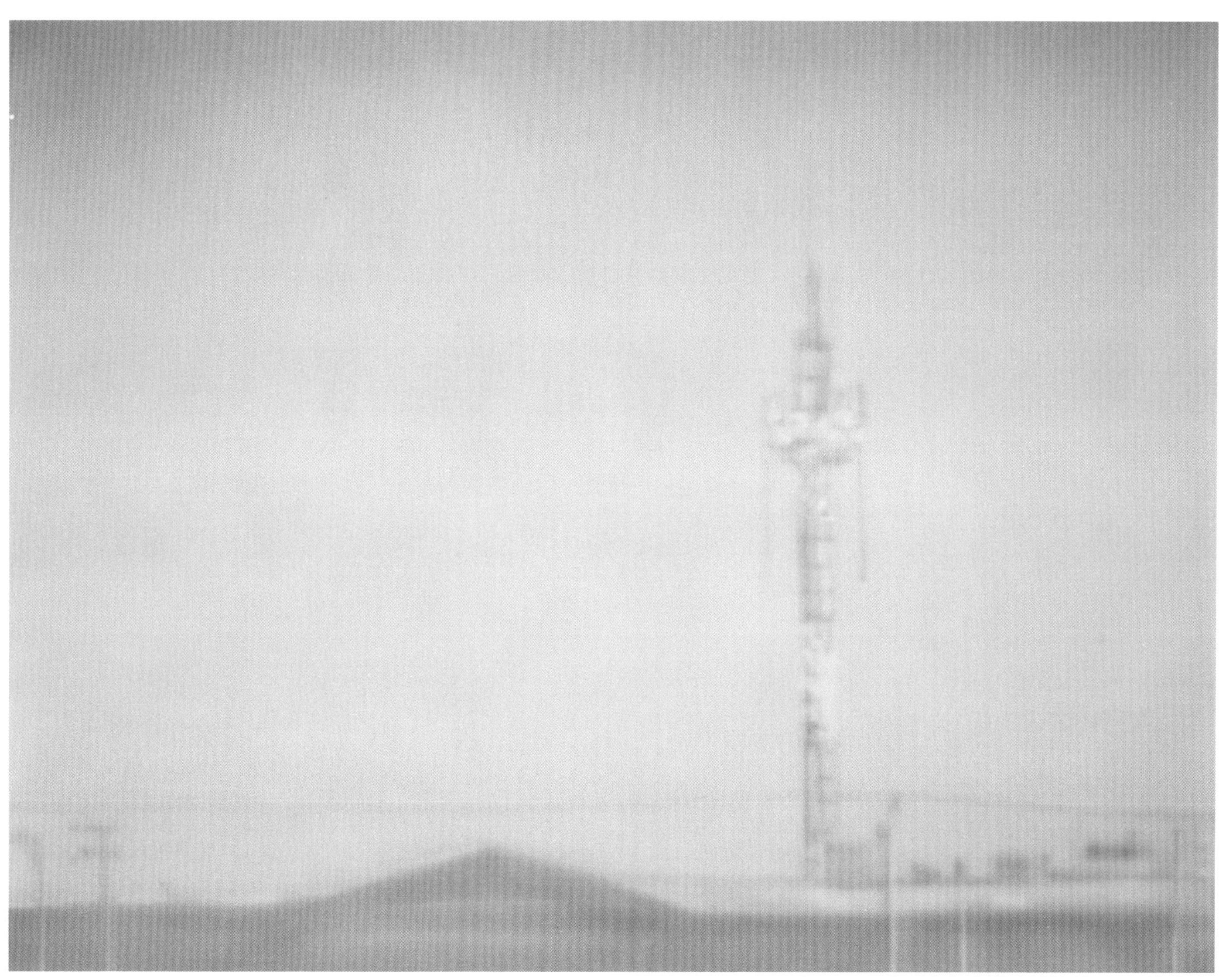

Parres 55 – 4, 2007. Acrylic enamel on MDF, 45 × 55 cm

Non-Places

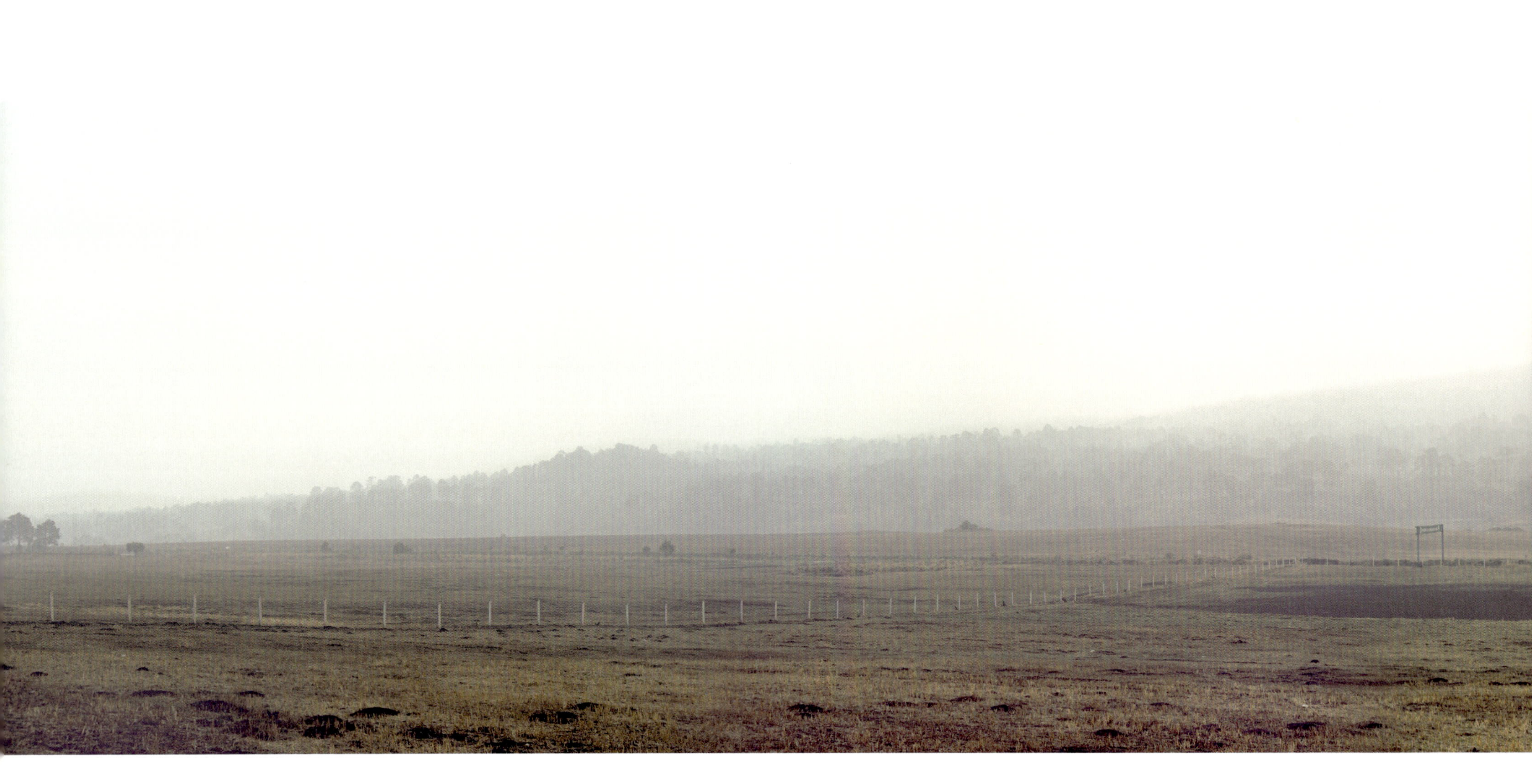

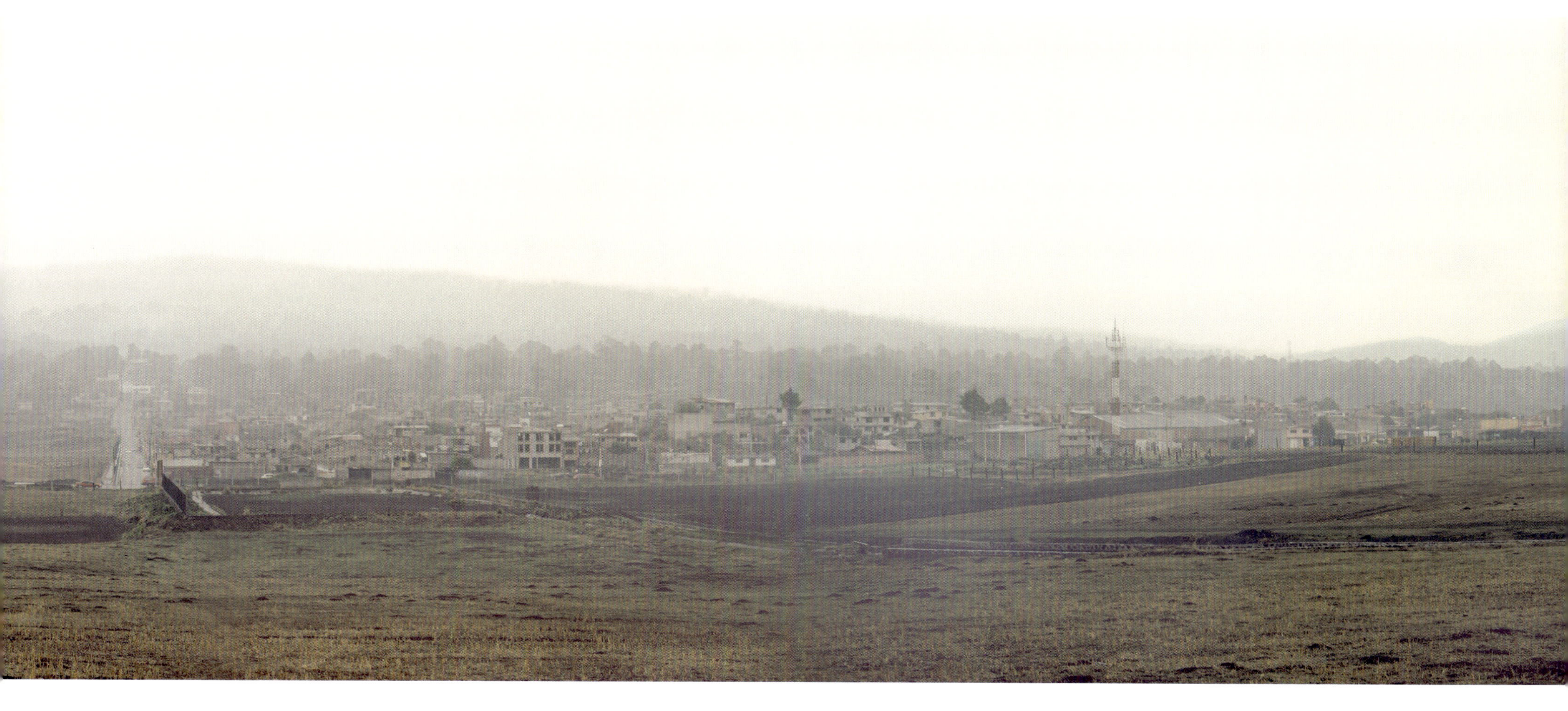

Parres landscape, 2006. Digital photo

Before 1975, there are almost no written records of the "rural village" of Parres-La Guarda in the municipality of Tlalpan of the Federal District (Mexico City), located at the 39.8-kilometer marker of the Mexico City-Cuernavaca highway. There is no pre-Hispanic settlement on the maps drawn in the 1950s by linguist Robert Barlow in his studies of the expanse of the Mexica (Aztec) Empire.[1] In the late nineteenth century, a Spanish entrepreneur, Castro de la Fuente Parres (written "Parras" in some documents), established an inn or posada as a rest stop for travelers where coachmen could also change their carriages' mounts, at an equidistant point, high up in the mountains, between the two cities. The unnamed site became known as La Guarda, and this was also the name given to the small train station on the Mexico-Cuernavaca railroad that President Porfirio Díaz inaugurated in 1897, and that marked the end of the neighboring Posada de la Guarda's brief existence.

Over half a century later, in 1954, a sculpture was erected at km 39.8, a few hundred yards from the train station, to mark the highest point of the road.

It was an initiative of Pedro Ramírez Vázquez's, an architect working at the time for a certain "Trust of the Federal District," a futureless association that formed part of the Mexico City government led by Regent Ernesto P. Uruchurtu, known as "the northern barbarian" for his will to modernization: he cleared the way for avenues and expressways like the Periférico (or Ring Road) by demolishing entire neighborhoods, and built huge Quonset hut-like local markets in areas like Tepito and La Lagunilla; he was also a diehard reactionary, closing the city's most traditional and popular brothels, literary sources beyond compare.[2] One of Uruchurtu's many and always frantic schemes, perhaps his most elaborate one, was to melt the city into a "harmonious whole" and not let any marginal space escape his control. The rural area of Parres-La Guarda, with its wheat fields and sheep ranches scattered among the mountains, was one of these peripheral zones with deep Nahuatl roots that had to be incorporated without fail. Out of the adobe ruins of the Posada de la Guarda rose a primary school, with a good-sized yard and a couple of classrooms in what had been the stables. The scheme worked: the isolated mountain inhabitants were gradually drawn to the school and ended up settling around it for purely practical reasons.[3]

It is not quite clear what came first: the school or the statue. I am inclined to think that the statue came first and that the school opened later, though it did not do very well in the beginning, since it was re-inaugurated in 1995.

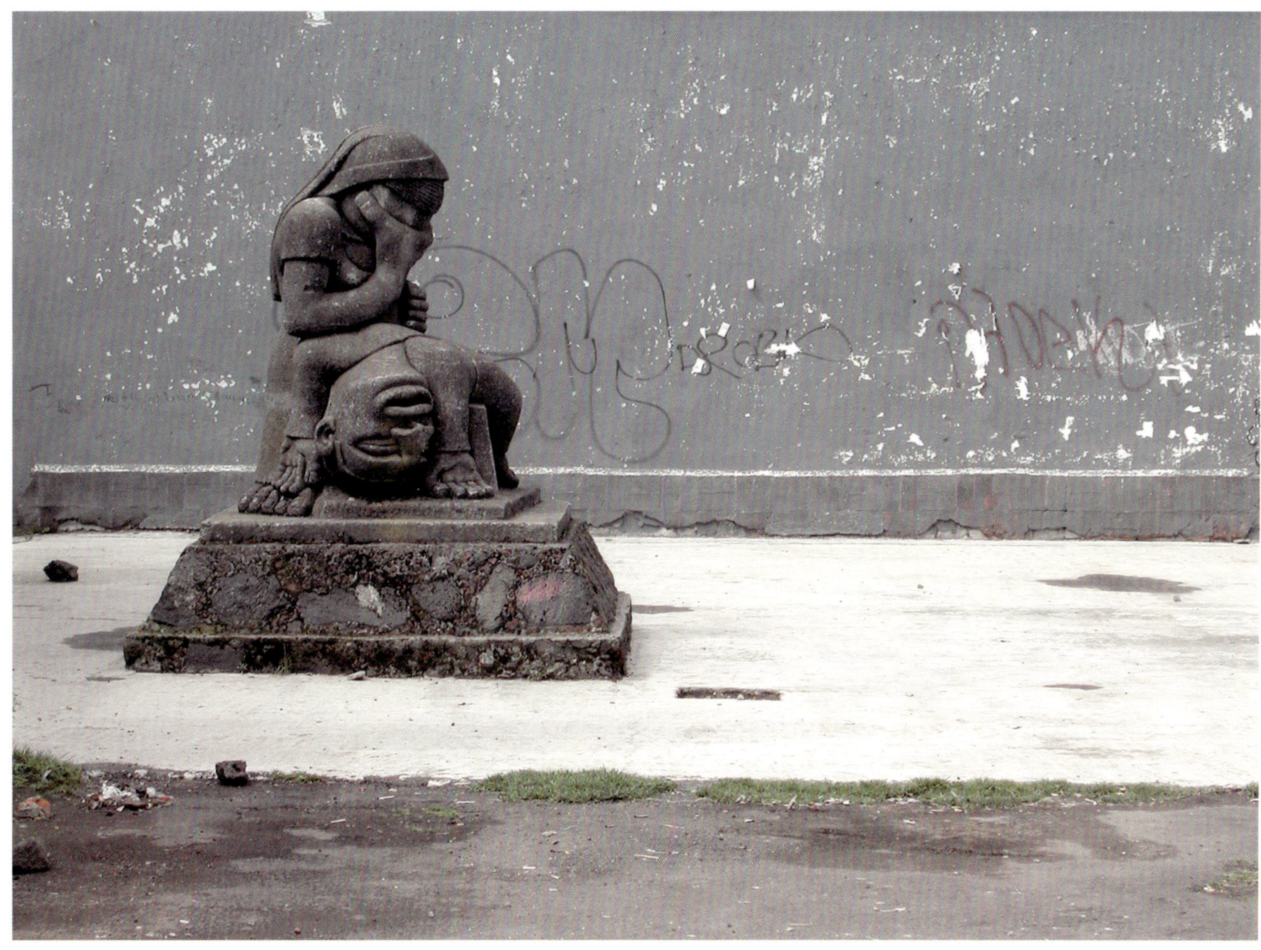

Francisco Marin, *Campesino sacrificado* (Sacrificed Peasant), 1954. Situated on the roadside in Parres

The piece from 1954, *Campesino sacrificado* (Sacrificed Peasant), by Francisco Marín (a doctor by profession and Diego Rivera's brother-in-law) is a late example – at a time when the dominant tendency in sculpture was modern and abstract – of a monumental style that evolved in the shadow of Muralism and the Escuela de Talla Directa (Direct Carving School); its main proponents were Oliverio Martínez (who made the sculptures for the Monument to the Revolution in 1935), Carlos Bracho and Luis Ortiz Monasterio. Marín's patriotic pietà depicts a subject rooted in post-revolutionary Mexican culture: the violent death of a peasant whose blood fertilizes barren ground, represented in Rivera's early frescos *La liberación del peón* (The Peon's Liberation), 1923, at the headquarters of the Public Education Department, repeated in his series of murals at Chapingo University) and, in the end, fairly well adapted to these whereabouts, which had once been the stomping grounds of Zapata loyalists and the route that the revolutionary leader and his generals had taken into Mexico City in 1915.[4] Less allegorical or contrived than the works of Ortiz Monasterio or Bracho, *Campesino sacrificado* recoups and summarizes many of the lessons of the Escuela de Talla Directa (for instance, a massive appearance totally opposed to Brancusi's slender elegance), though in its broad round shapes it already bears the mark of Henry Moore. As critic Antonio Luna Arroyo pointed out in 1964, Marín was above all an intimist sculptor, better skilled at making busts.[5] In fact, *Campesino sacrificado* as well as *Duelo por Zapata* (Mourning for Zapata), which it resembles, are atypical pieces in Marín's body of work, though – if we are to believe Diego Rivera – these "sculptures of the Anahuac"[6] were created by the artist of his own volition and not as the result of an official commission.[7]

When *Campesino sacrificado* was put in place beside the Mexico City-Cuernavaca highway – where traffic was increasing as ruling-party bigwigs built weekend homes in the "city of eternal spring," where they enjoyed rubbing shoulders with princesses from Savoy or Hollywood actresses (Helen Hayes, etc.) – the town of Parres did not yet exist. According to all the reports, the sculpture was simply placed "at km 39.8" without even a mention of the train station, which seems to have been practically forgotten by then.[8]

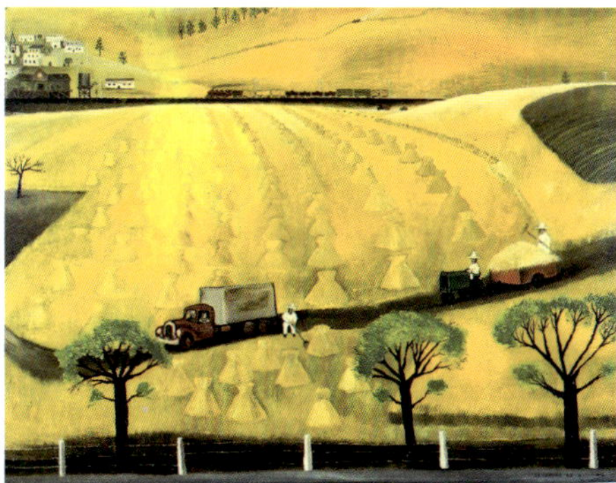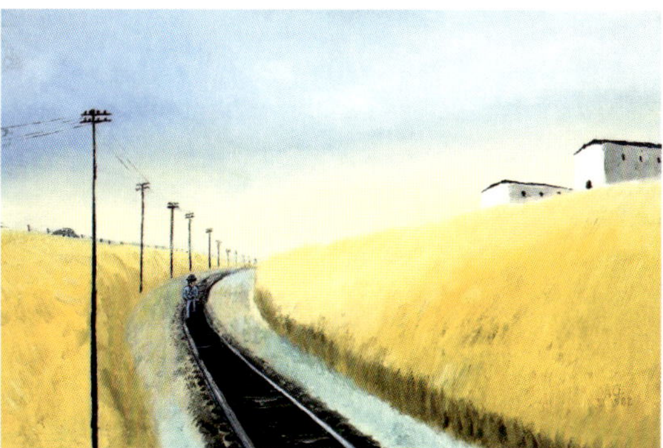

The town's name – indistinctly Parres or La Guarda – begins to appear in print in the 1970s due to the demonstrations of communal landowners from the municipality of Milpa Alta, situated some sixteen kilometers east of it, as they fought to conserve the stands of fir trees that were being cut down both legally and illegally on Cuauhtzin mountain – with a private army called the *monteros* – for the Loreto y Peña Pobre paper mill.[9] In those final years of President Luis Echeverría's rule (1970 – 1976), a rumor had spread throughout the volcanic mountain range south of Mexico City that there was a plan to transform the whole area between Milpa Alta and the Ajusco – including Parres, obviously – into a tourist zone, with hotels, amusement parks and cottages in countrified housing developments. It is not clear, however, how Parres began to acquire an urban appearance right at this time, counter to the prevailing trend. This high-altitude plain (almost 10,000 feet above sea level) devoted to agricultural activities that are unusual for the region (indeed, in the country as a whole), namely wheat cultivation and seasonal sheep pasturing, appeared (and continues to appear) rather heterodox in terms of the mythological configuration of Mexico and its imagery, easier to associate with the chilly scenery of the Alps or Pyrenees than with the tropical clichés of Tehuantepec or Yucatán. This is the nostalgic memory of cartoonist and painter Abel Quezada, who in the 1970s painted various landscapes of the Parres area in August, when conical bales of hay create a golden grid over the rolling fields surrounded by thick evergreen forest.

Some architectural remains lead us to believe that some of the land in Parres was purchased, probably in the 1970s, for summer homes, possibly as the first step in the transformation of the area into a tourist zone (where Nahuatl names would provide quaint historic reminders): roomy houses with gabled, shingle roofs, a view of the lovely forested landscape of the Pelado Volcano, and at their backs, the Autopista del Sol (the Mexico City-Acapulco toll highway, opened in 1967). When and why, then, did Parres grow, not as an upper-middle-class residential area, but as a kind of free-floating simulacrum of the urban sprawl that, in those years, was encroaching upon the Chalco Valley, Iztapalapa, Ciudad Nezahualcóyotl and Santa Fe? Separating Parres from the southernmost edge of Mexico City's slums, there are still,

Left: Abel Quezada, *La Cosecha* (The Harvest), 1975. Oil on canvas, 100 × 124 cm
Right: Abel Quezada, *Vias del tren de Parres* (Train Tracks of Parres), 1983. Oil on canvas, 30 × 45 cm

in spite of illegal logging, twenty or more kilometers of woodland, with a scattering of rural farms and stables, only interrupted by an electrical substation and a waste processing plant outside of Topilejo.

Nonetheless, travelers to Parres will find the same brutal architecture that the economic crises of the 1980s and 90s left behind on the outskirts of so many historic towns, or in the kinds of suburbs that were called "lost cities" not so long ago but have recently been euphemistically rechristened "marginal areas": windowless grey cinderblock walls, sometimes smeared with a telltale coating of pastel yellow, pink, or blue paint, with rebar sprouting out at the top, waiting to anchor a second story that will never be built and inevitably tipped with an upside-down beer bottle like a makeshift lightning rod; streets that, though they might already have names, are just rough dirt beaten down by tractors and trucks; and dogs that, parodying Flaubert's dictionary, can bear no other adjective except "starving."

With 3 million inhabitants in 1975, Ciudad Nezahualcóyotl, situated in the dry Texcoco lakebed abutting Mexico City limits, had already caught the eye of political parties who understood its enormous vote potential (and, to a lesser extent, the need to defuse a potential hotbed of urban upheaval); they spent much time and effort, investing heavily and launching social programs, to transform this huge unplanned settlement into a suburb equipped with services, schools, parks, cultural centers, and even sculptures by famous artists (Vicente Rojo). Troubled areas on the outskirts of other Mexican cities (Tijuana, Ciudad Juárez) benefited from the experience garnered in "Neza" (as it is popularly known). But Parres-La Guarda already had its monument, and its 300-odd inhabitants did not represent a big enough pool of votes to any party, so no one gave a damn about them.

Parres has no church but it does have a square, where vendors sell *barbacoa*, and an ugly kiosk with a corrugated metal roof, where the town's brass band rehearses and where shows take place whenever the Mexico City Department of Culture bothers to send performers – i.e., once in a blue moon. The primary school occupies a lot surrounded by ancient adobe walls: all that remains of the Posada de la Guarda; the closest secondary school and clinic are twenty kilometers away in Topilejo.

Though it is located in a region with heavy rainfall and is, more often than not, shrouded for most of the day in fog, Parres only has one well; its inhabitants get their drinking water piped in from the nearby state of Morelos – at an outrageous price, almost 3000% what the Mexico City government charges for water.

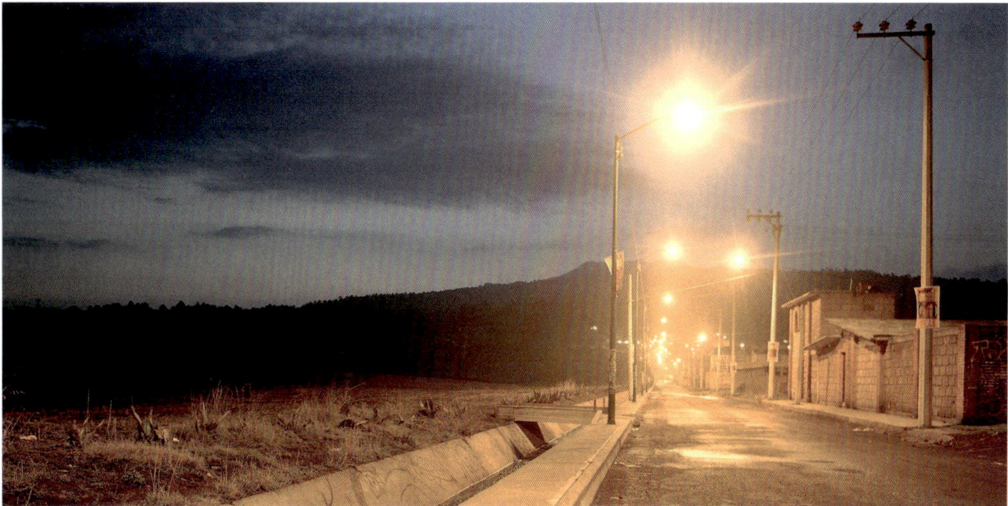

In Parres you can buy seed, fertilizer, spare parts for John Deere tractors, beer, and *barbacoa*. You have to go into the city – to the closest Wal-Mart – for everything else.

There is a cemetery in Parres, in a glen beside a swampy area that splits the town in two, lending it the shape, on a map or on Google Earth, of butterfly wings.

Francisco Marín's statue now stands on the exact spot where these two wings would join over the highway, but any notion of its revolutionary origin has been forgotten: nowadays, as dates have become blurred and the more elaborate identitarian signs of post-revolutionary Mexico add to the confusion, it is known in the town as "the monument to the man run over by a car," perhaps commemorating some other equally blurry episode in Parres's brief history.

Parres has grown over the last thirty years without quite knowing why or how; maybe it aspires to be linked some day to the Autopista del Sol that outlines the horizon like a mirage of modernity – a constant flow of lights of BMWs, Mercedes, and Audis, as recognizable airplane tail-lights, at 180 km/hr – or maybe it secretly hopes that urban sprawl will catch up to it some day.

In his book *Planet of Slums*, Mike Davis suggests that it is no longer the inhabitants of rural areas that migrate to cities, but rather the cities that migrate to them, incorporating the rural within the

Dawn view of Parres, 2006

urban and even establishing "new routes" that re-determine the economic activities and vocation of a community.[10] Parres – at least in its purely conceptual (and architectural) aspects – could exemplify this theory, but it does not, and might even contradict it: Parres is at once too far and too close to the city to belong to the sphere of "migrant communities" since it never had its *moment*: it did not have it in the 1960s when the highway was built 150 meters from the *Campesino sacrificado* that, in Parres's memory, has come to acknowledge an accident that no one remembers; nor did it have it in the 1970s, when Mexico City witnessed explosive growth; nor will it have it now, since both the federal government and the Mexico City government declared it would be a "protected area" and "wildlife reserve," thwarting any possibility of change: the town can neither revert to a former, idealized pastoral state, nor integrate itself into the urban sprawl and hence, into the "social body" of a city to which it nonetheless belongs politically.

Parres, characterized as one of the seventeen (and most eccentric) "rural towns" of the Federal District, is a historical absurdity – and yet a definitely exemplary one – which came to a stop at some imprecise moment between 1970 and 2000. Parres's non-time determines its non-place: it is not the utopia of the Enlightenment, because the latter did indeed have a reason for being in the Western imaginary insofar as it defined, by subtraction, a certain concept of the urban and the social functions of the secular city within an ideal of progress that, paradoxically, must come to a stop at the moment of its fulfillment (this is the ideological foundation of both capitalism and socialism). Parres, in its atrocious – and atrophying – physicality, ground to a halt in the immanent present of all illusions.

Olivier Debroise

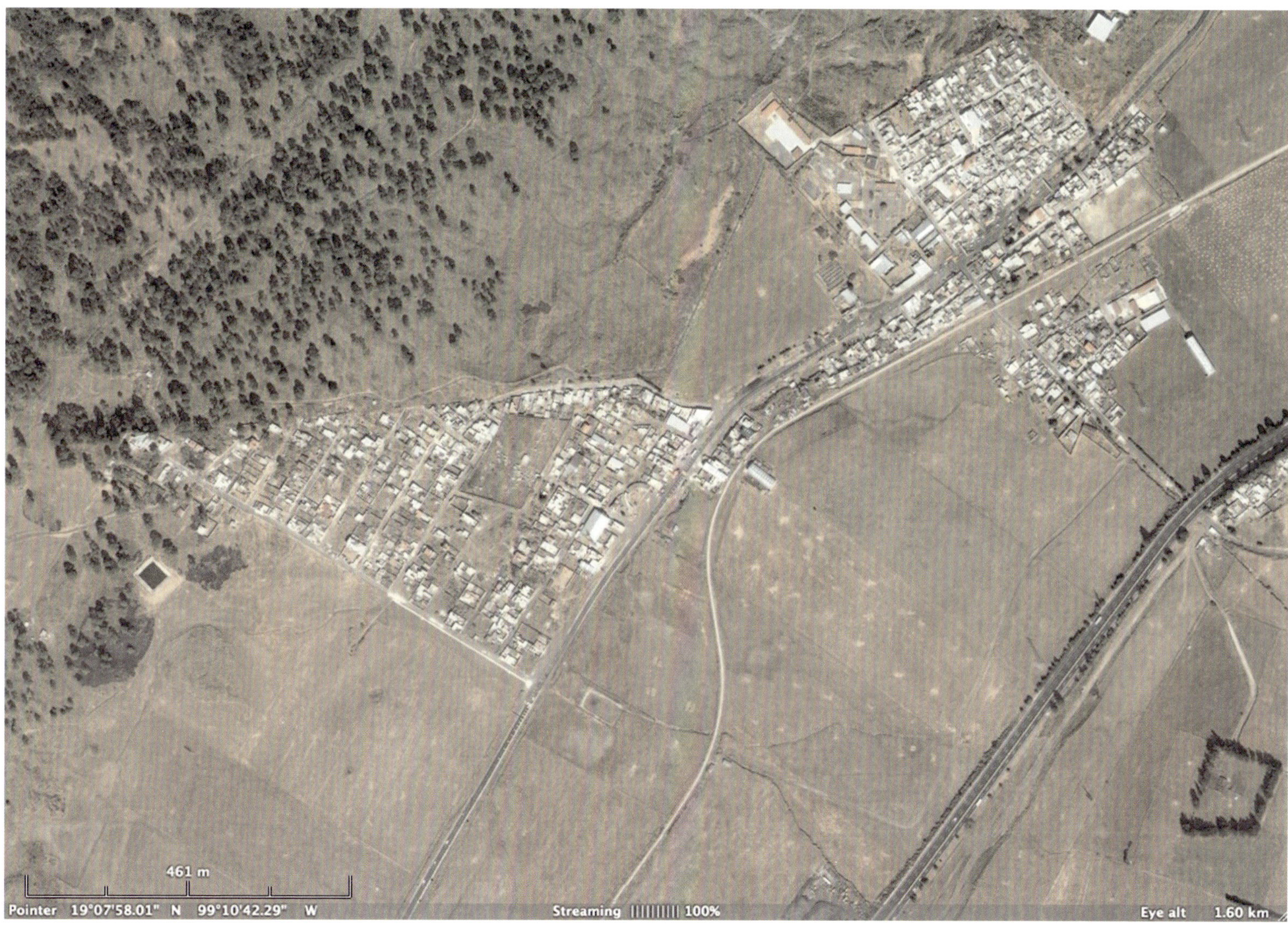

Google™ Earth map of Parres

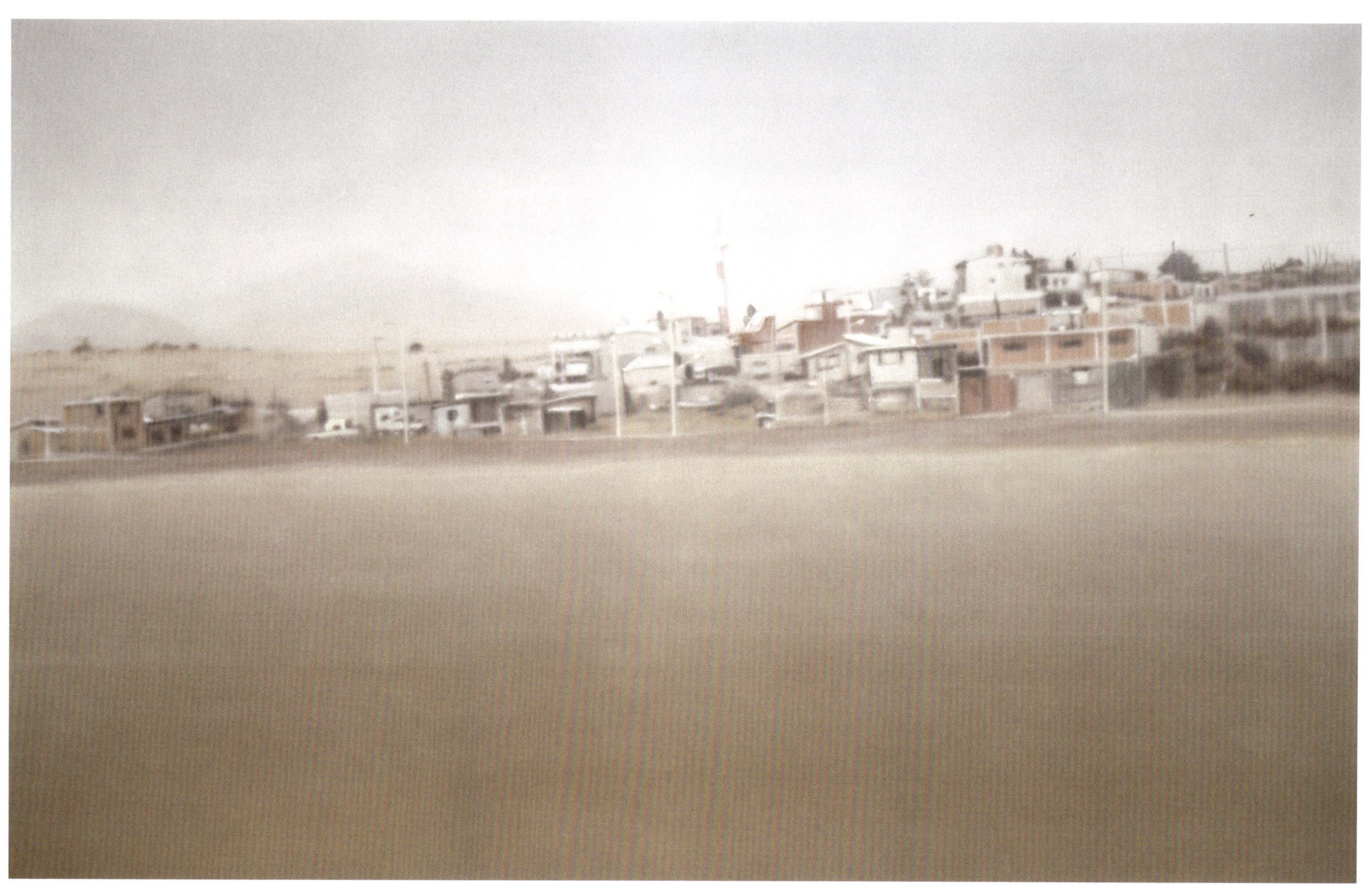

Parres 3, 2005. Acrylic enamel on acrylic, 130 × 200 cm

Parres is a series of projects using cinema's fundamental unit, the roll of film. In the historical development of film, the one roll take was, primarily, an attempt to capture reality in its unequivocal time frame. This continued in its limitless possibilities, until the first physical cut in the roll marked the beginning of both cinematic language, and time elipsis.

In *Parres 0* the premise is to use only the simplest mechanics of producing a moving image. 2067 still frames, when projected at 24 frames per second, are compacted into one roll of film which lasts 86 seconds. Instead of using the roll of film as a real time sequence, the camera is used as a still camera, in which every frame is a different still photograph, which in turn join into a long series of collages depicting the town through night and day, mist and sun, sadness and beauty. *Parres 0* became the memory of the unmemorable.

The Parres series deliberately includes both the tail end rolls of film, which mark the beginning and end of the physicality of the material, and hinting at the construction and break down of illusion.

Parres sets up a utopia of detachment, whilst bridging film and painting.

Parres alludes to the symbolic space brought about by the self-reflexivity of painting.

Parres III returns the visibility, masked by *Parres I*. It reveals the failure of broken promises.

Parres II is me at home.

Parres' monochrome becomes the systematic disappearance of the visible world in its everyday form.

Melanie Smith and Rafael Ortega

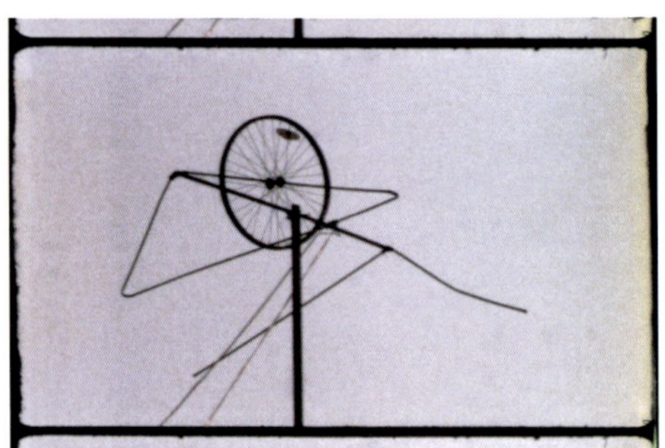
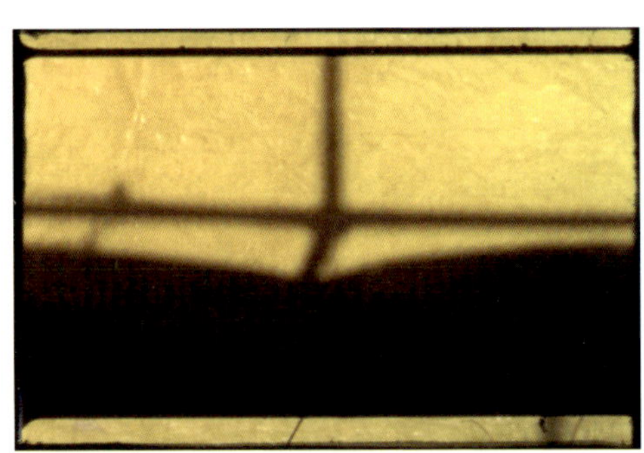
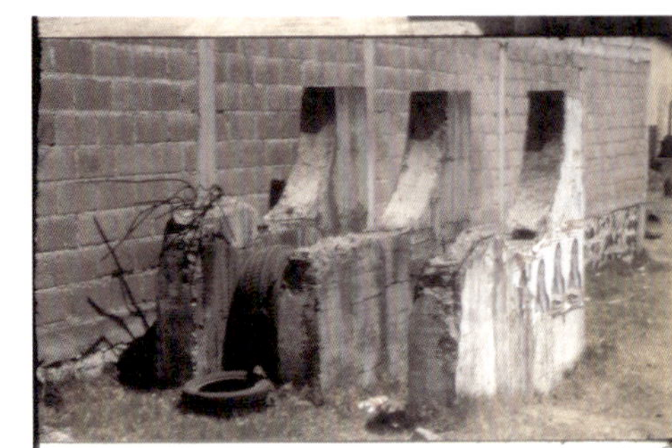
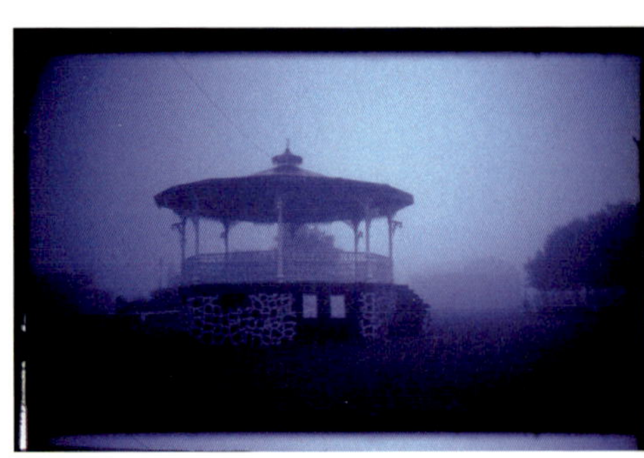
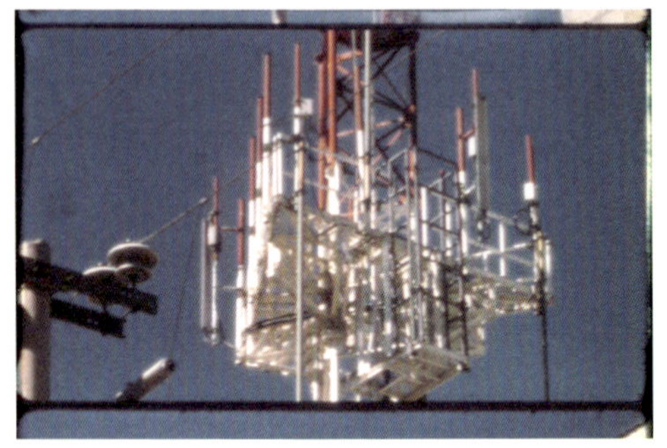
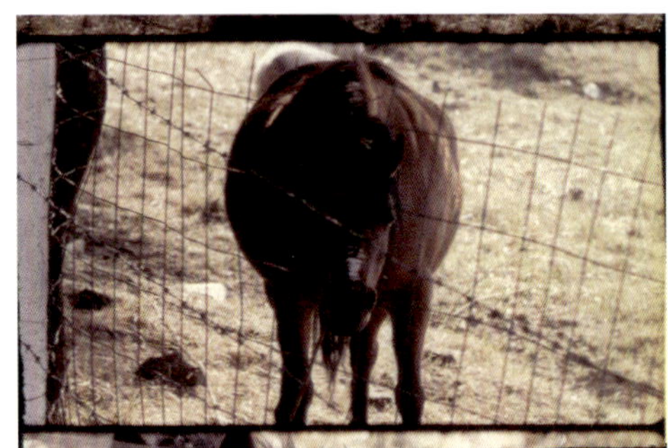
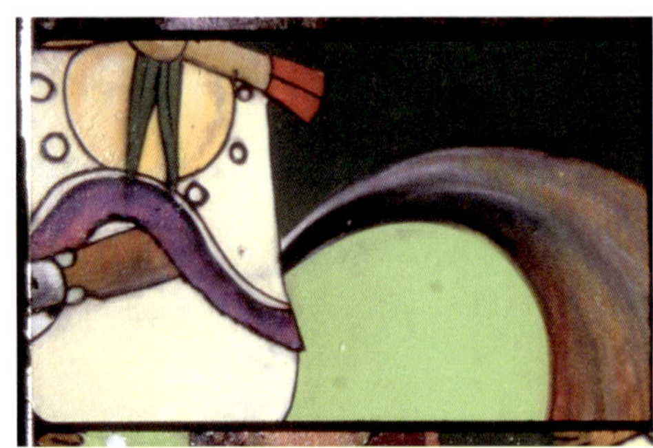
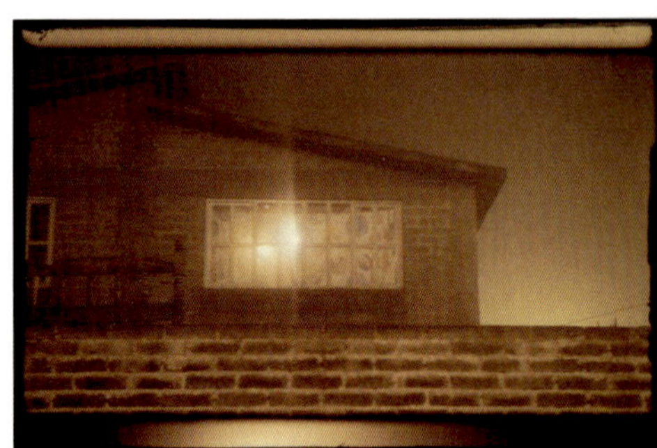

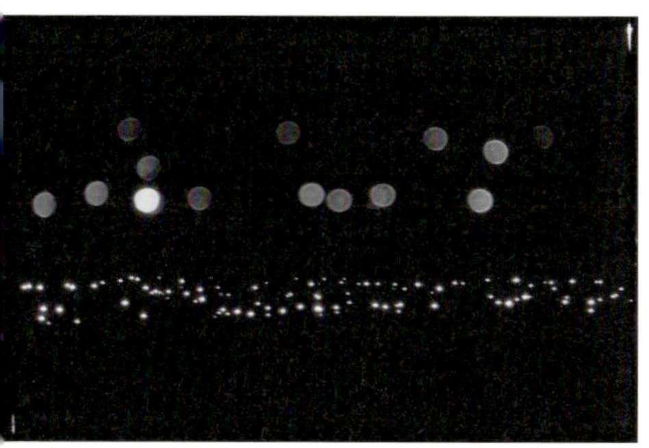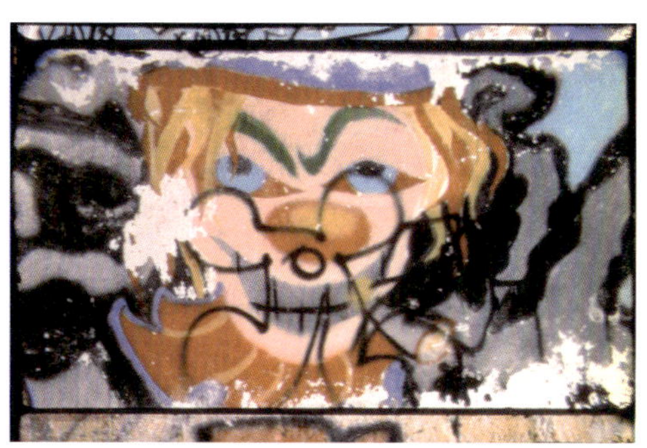
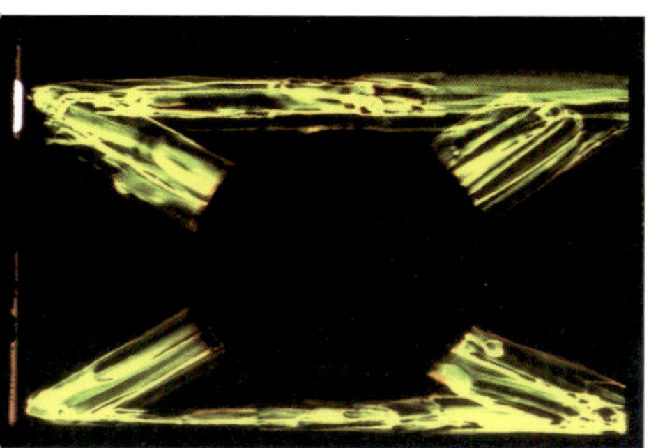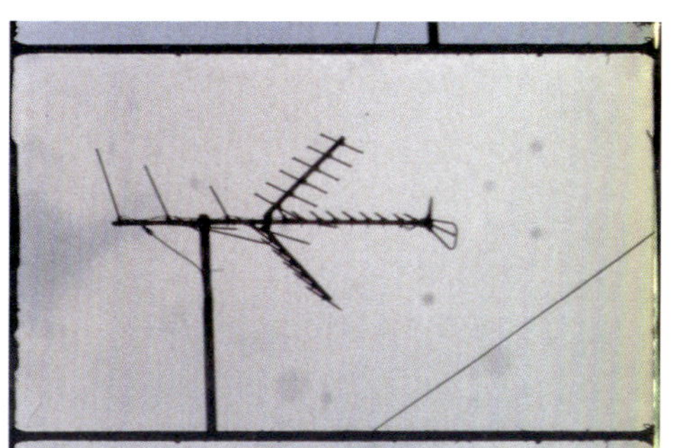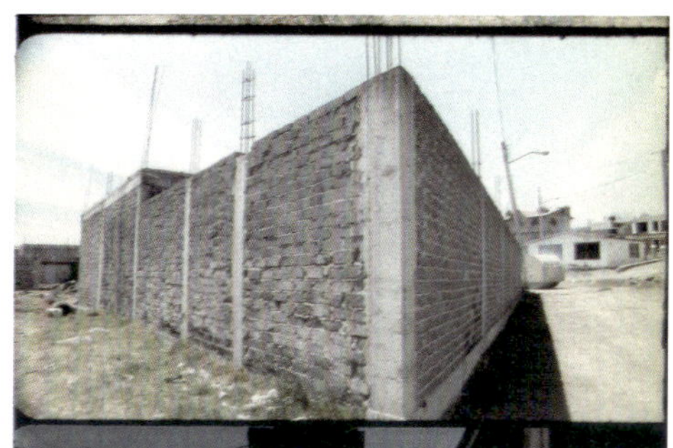

16 film still frames from the video *Parres 0*. (86-second film composed of 2067 different images.)

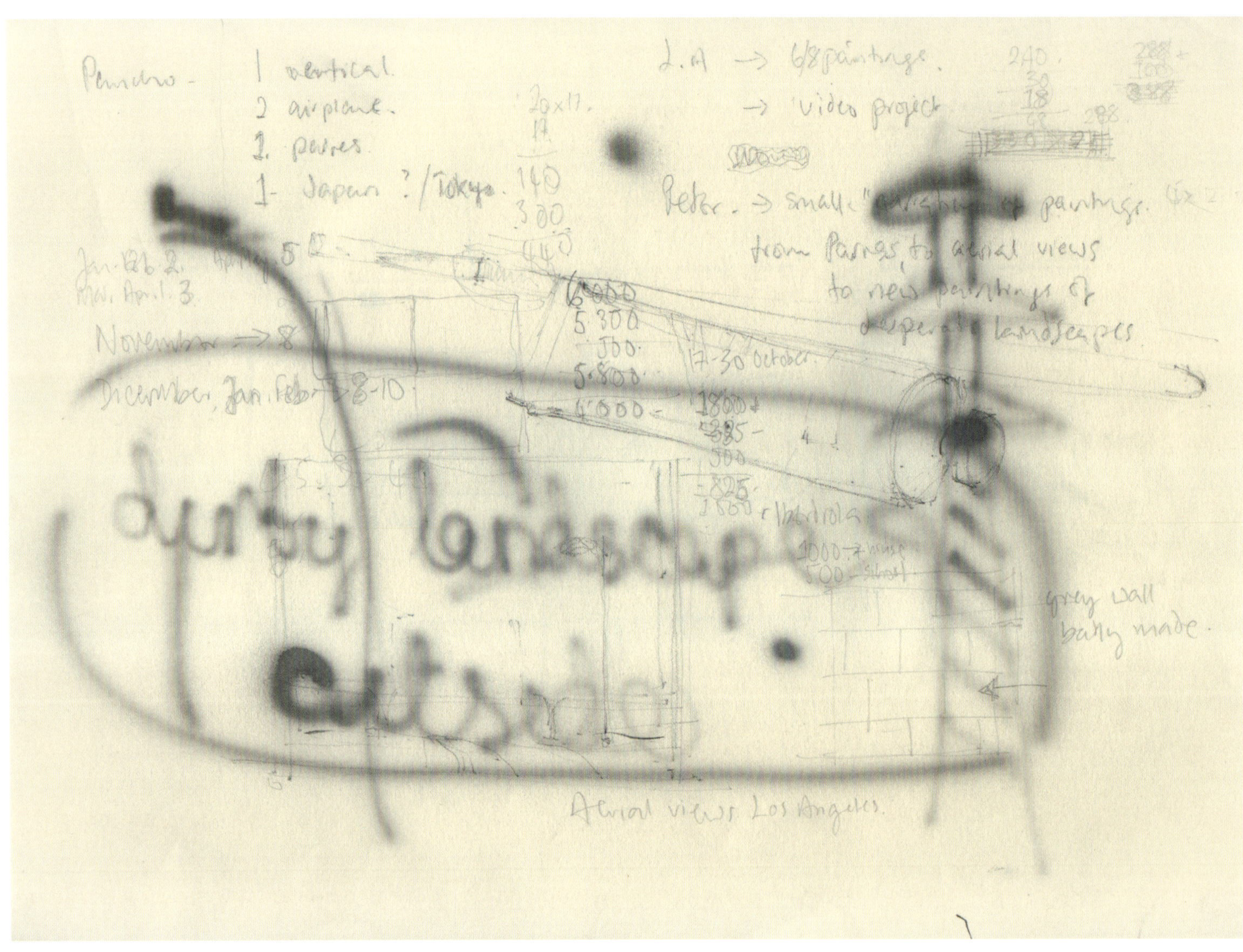

Drawing from notebook, 2006

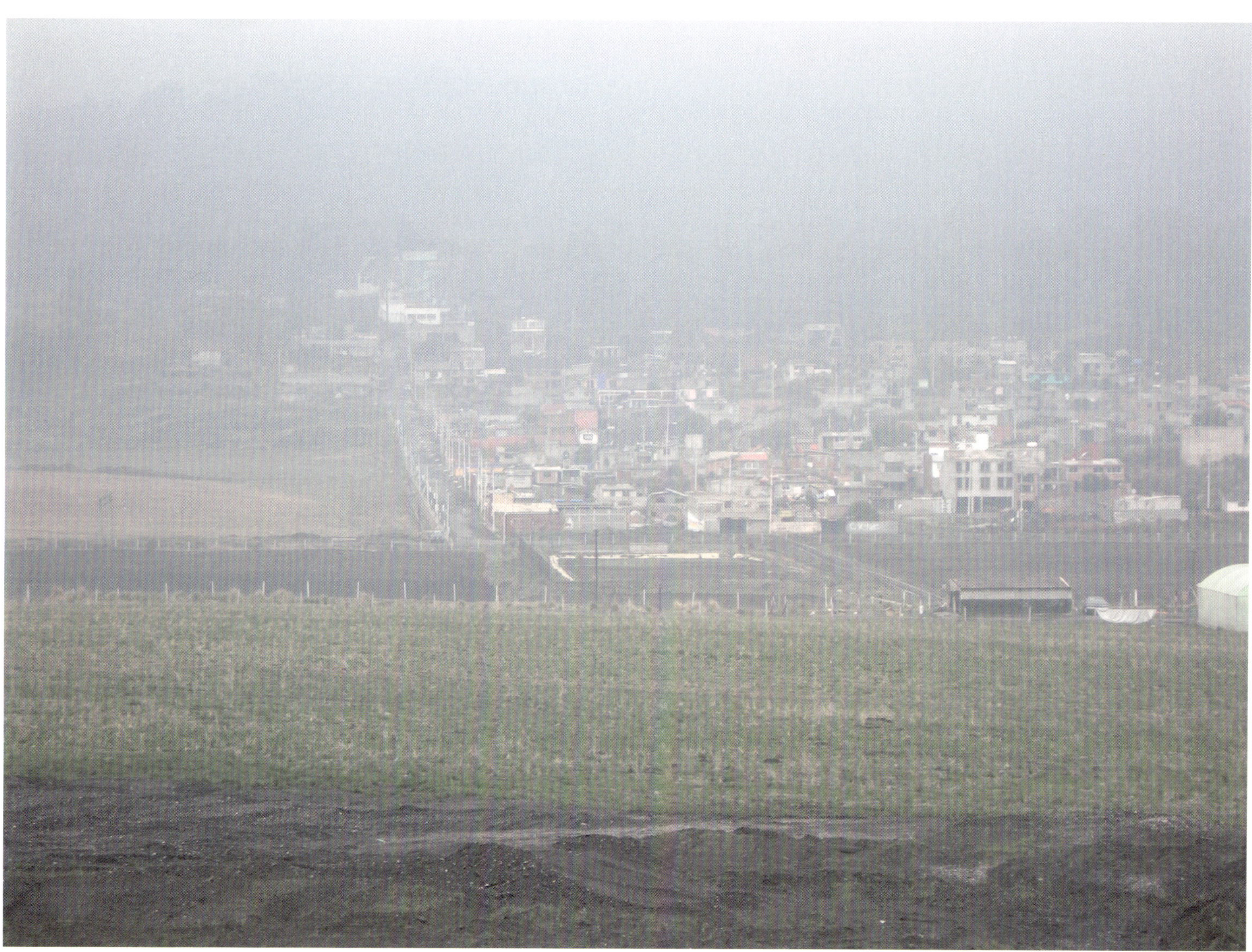

View of Parres. Digital print

Parres

The man in *Parres I* walks away from the city residences into a desolate patch of earth and begins painting. Here city is the opposite of painting and not the opposite of nature, as the history of Western thought would have it. City and painting become the new archetypical adversaries, with an operatic soundtrack lending a wistful air to this uncertain encounter between the real and the ideal.

Adam Lerner

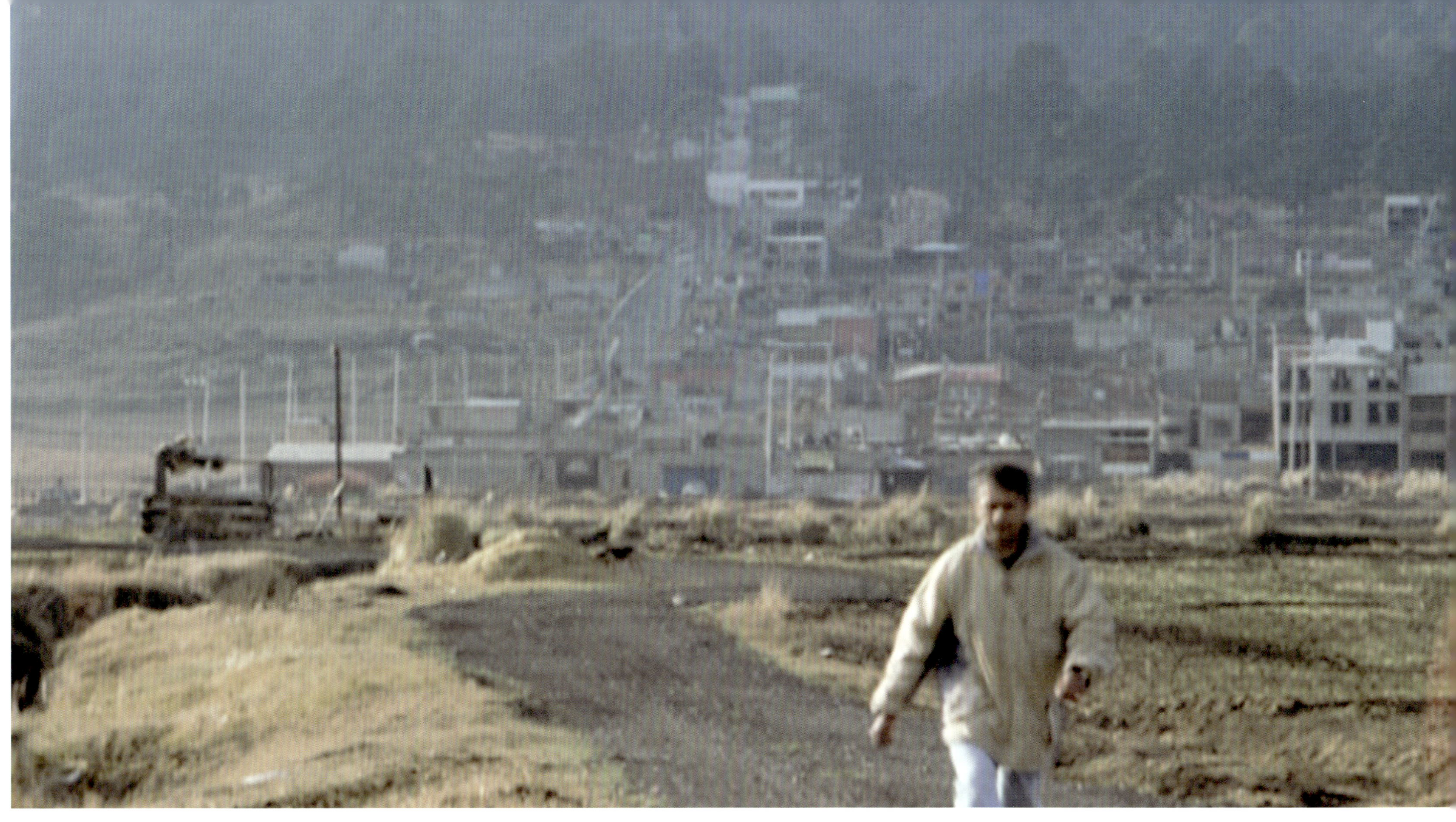

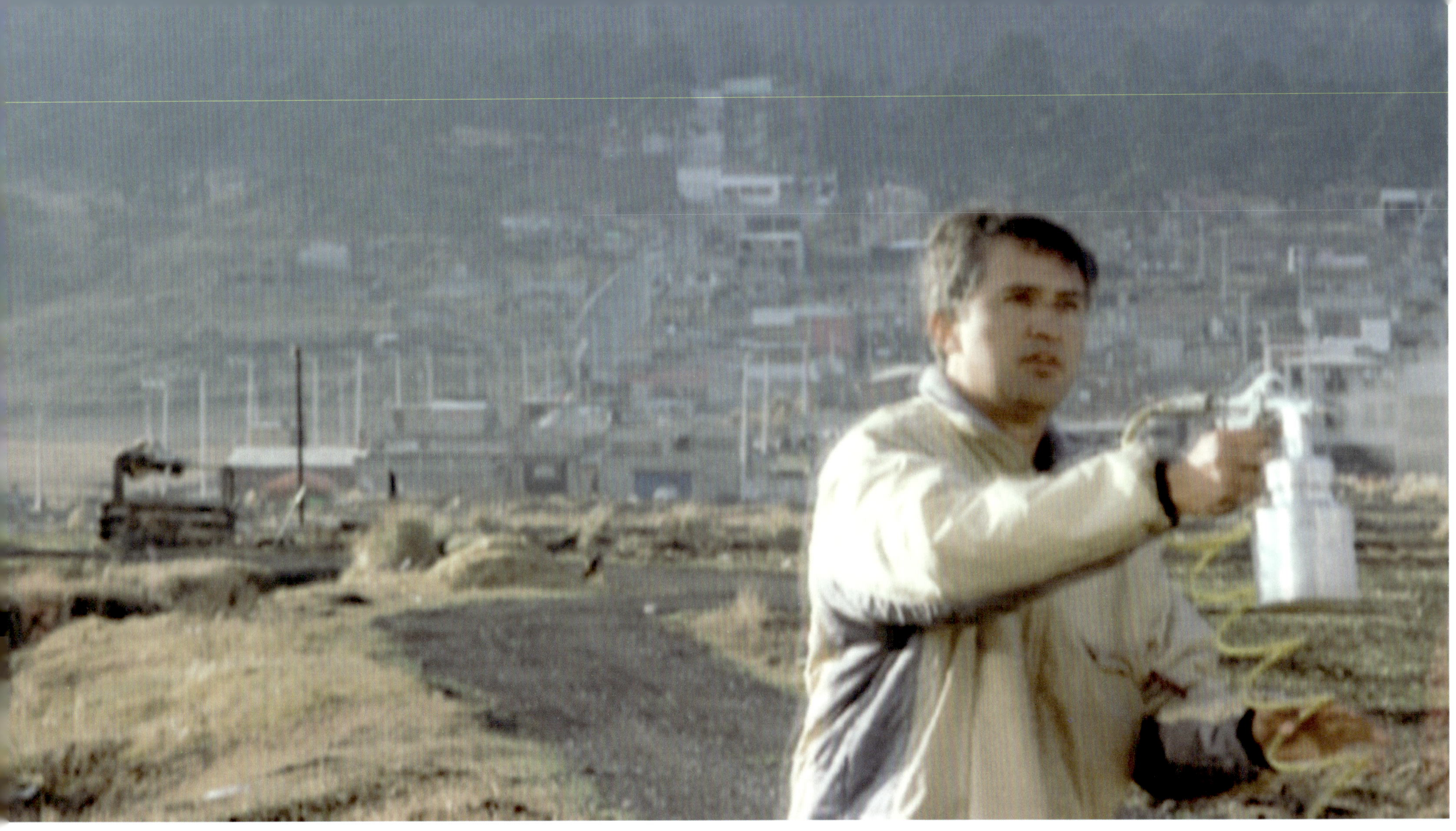

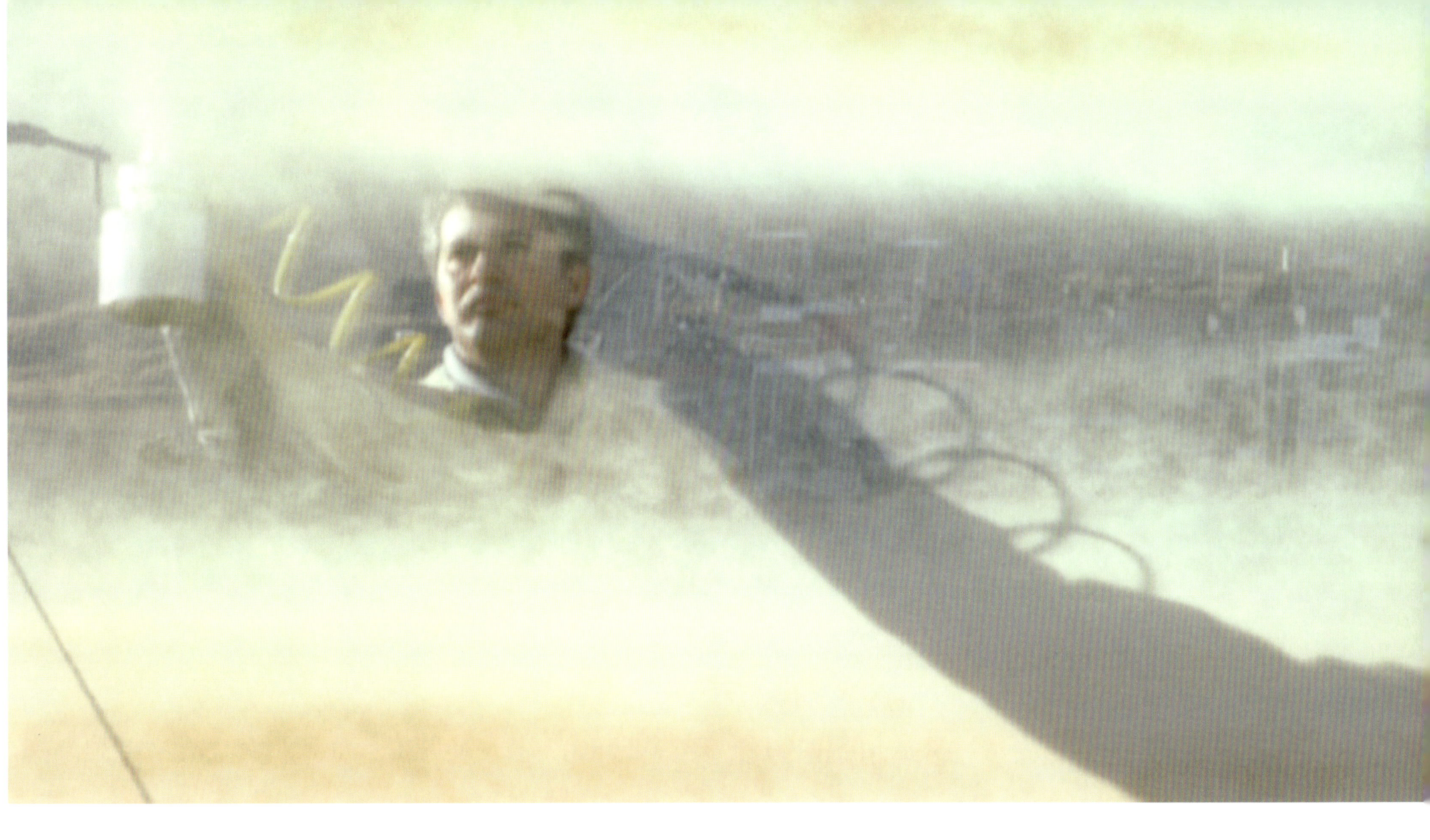

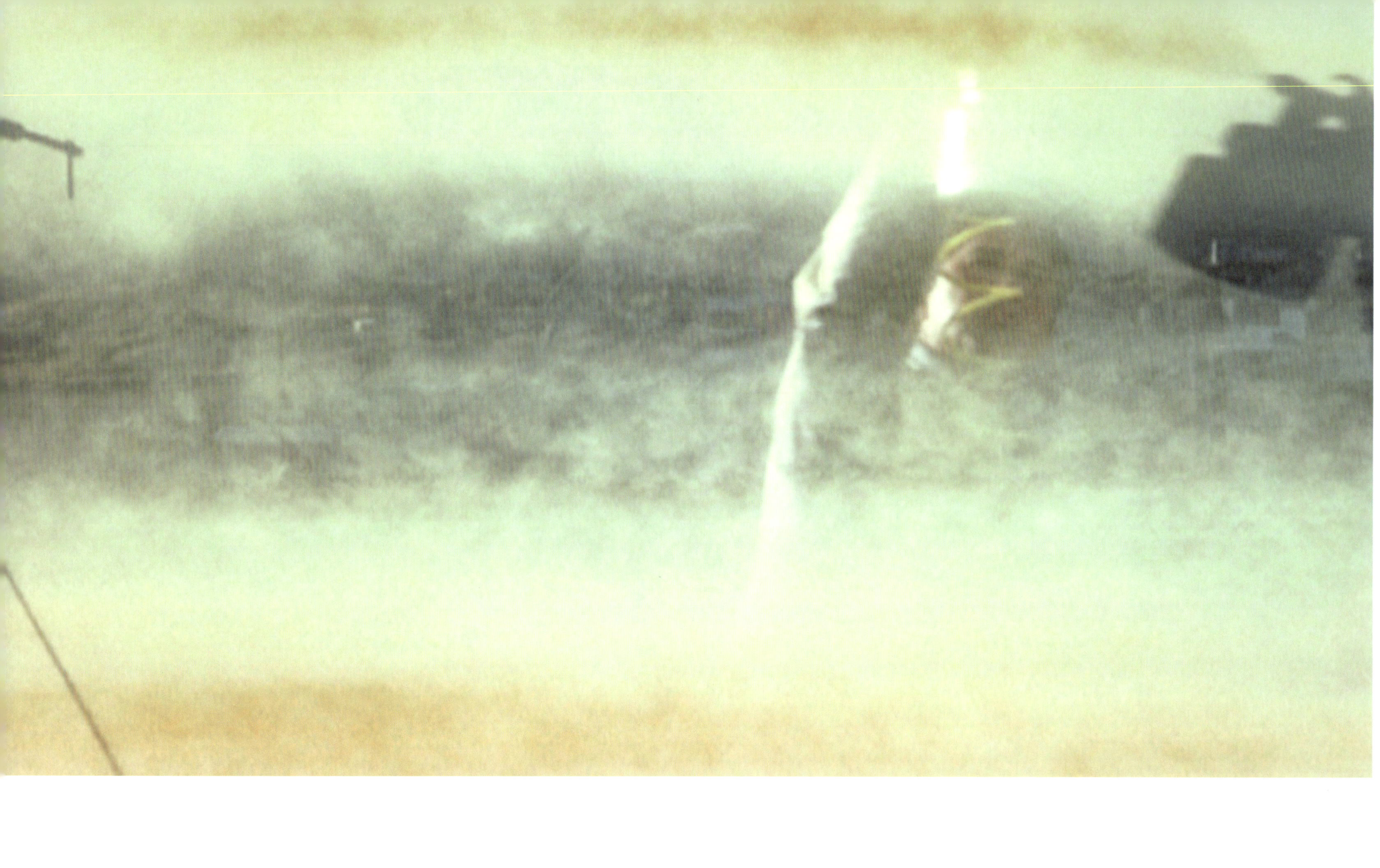

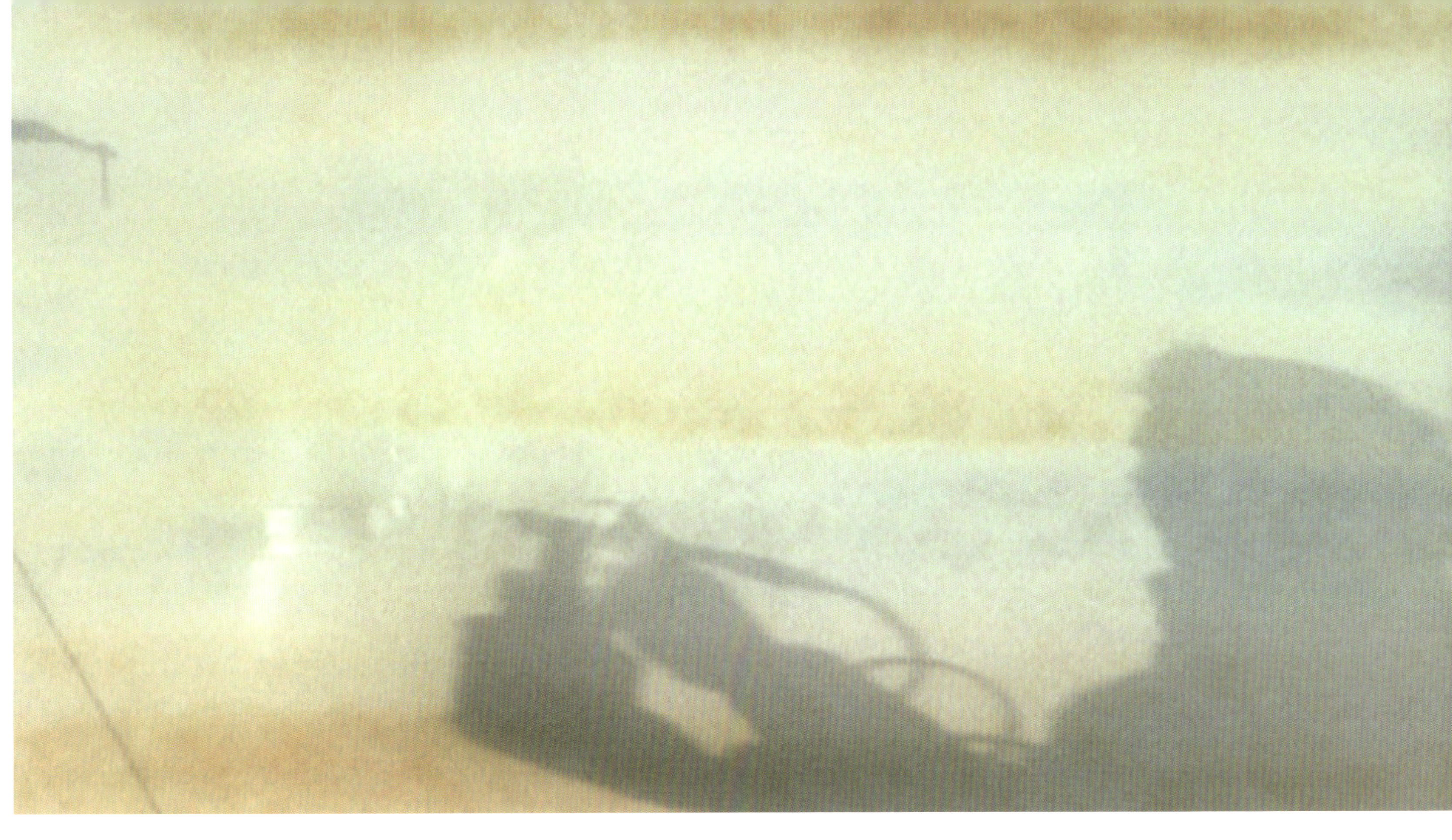

Stills from *Parres I*, 2004. 35mm transferred to DVD, 4 mins. 20 secs.

I'm Scottish and I live in Scotland. So (but? – the schizophrenia of the Scottish character will out…) – I like rain. I don't hold anything against the rain. Rain and wind together maybe. Incessant rain possibly. But not rain on its own.

And not the kind of rain in *Parres II* which speaks to me of days when things can happen because the sun hasn't drained every ounce of energy from limb and lip; which dribbles down bare legs and runs into sandshoes; which flickers when the sun shines.

My love of this rain links me, my mother told me, with my long gone but much loved grandmother, who when young loved to walk in this rain, through hill and dip, in a part of Scotland's Western Isles so remote that at the turn of the twentieth century, they were re-moved/displaced/replanted 'for their own good'. The kind of place which come to us now in BBC 2 documentaries; as a history told in rhythm and note; in books about puffins, or the sea; in sepia coloured little square photos which look as odd to us now, as the stories they tell are distant; in conversations which make my blood's oxygen spark and flash inside in ways hard to describe…

These photos show serious faces staring back at a stranger hidden behind a lens, a lens which had the power to make people leave their homes. They look like you Melanie, in your unflinching gaze, your portrait painting stillness, both questioning and asserting, vulnerable yet stoic. All is laid bare and as truthful as the camera allows. You stand still as we are pulled back and away by time and distance and the need to shelter from the rain.

Lorraine Wilson

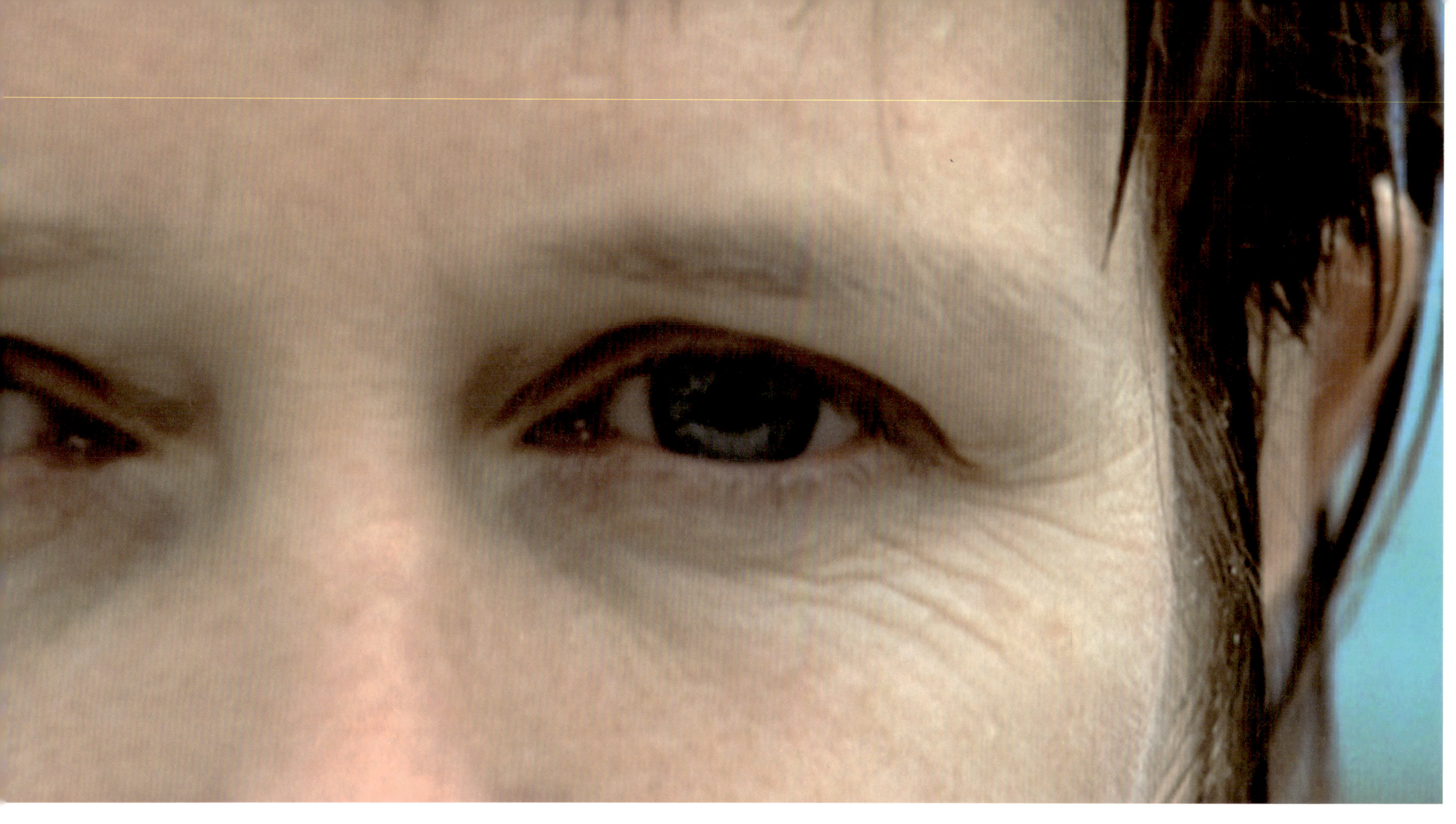

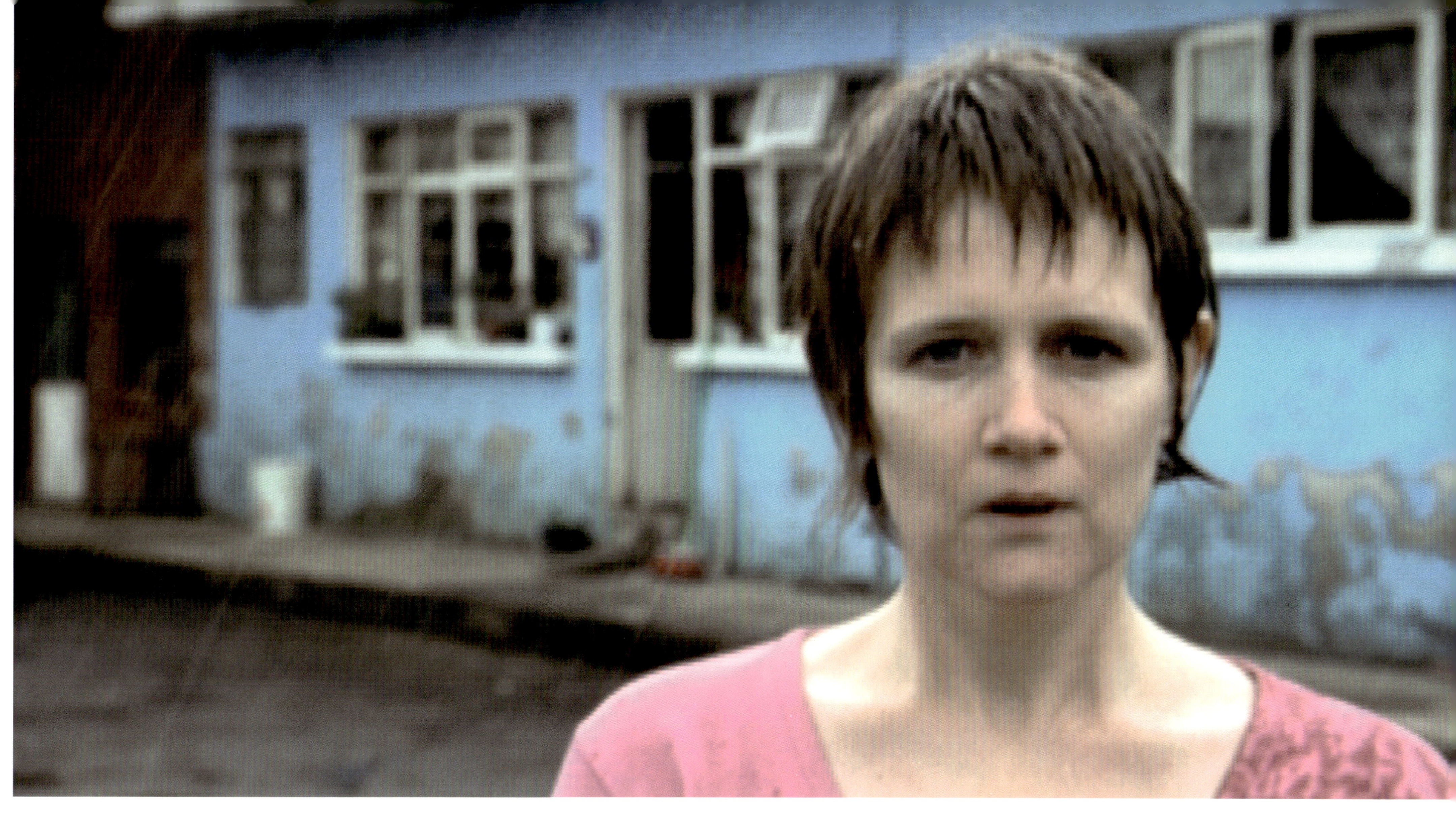

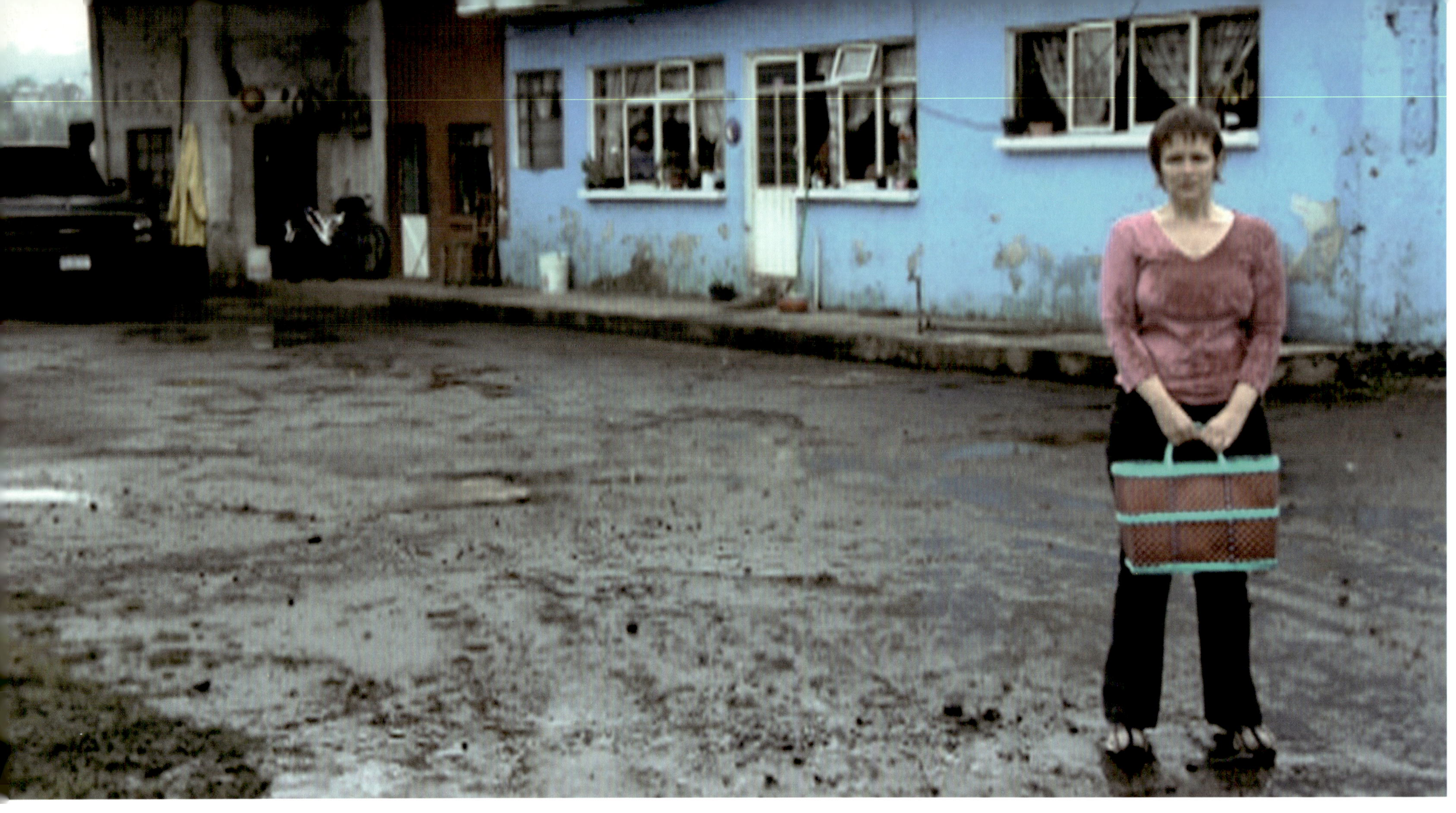

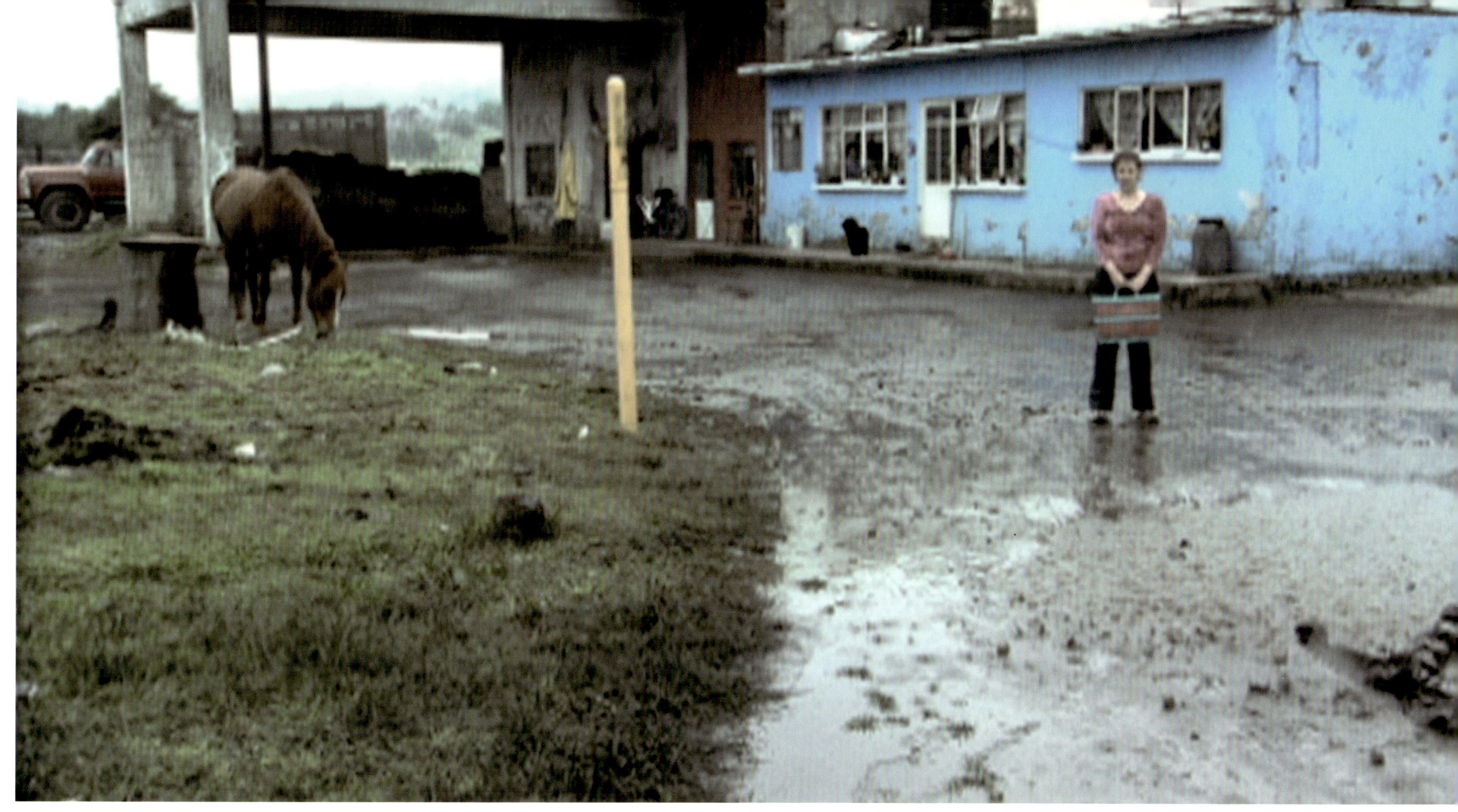

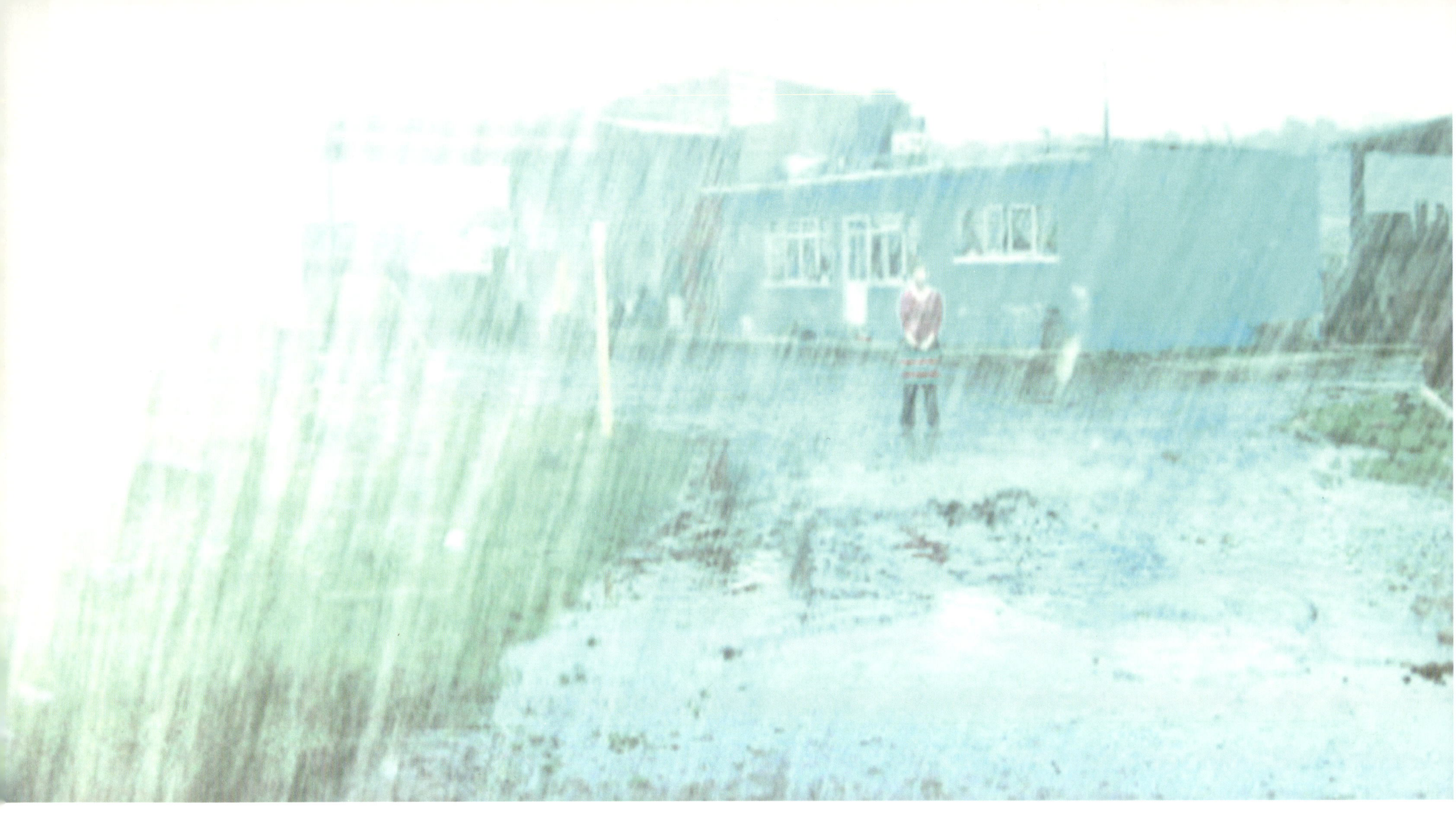

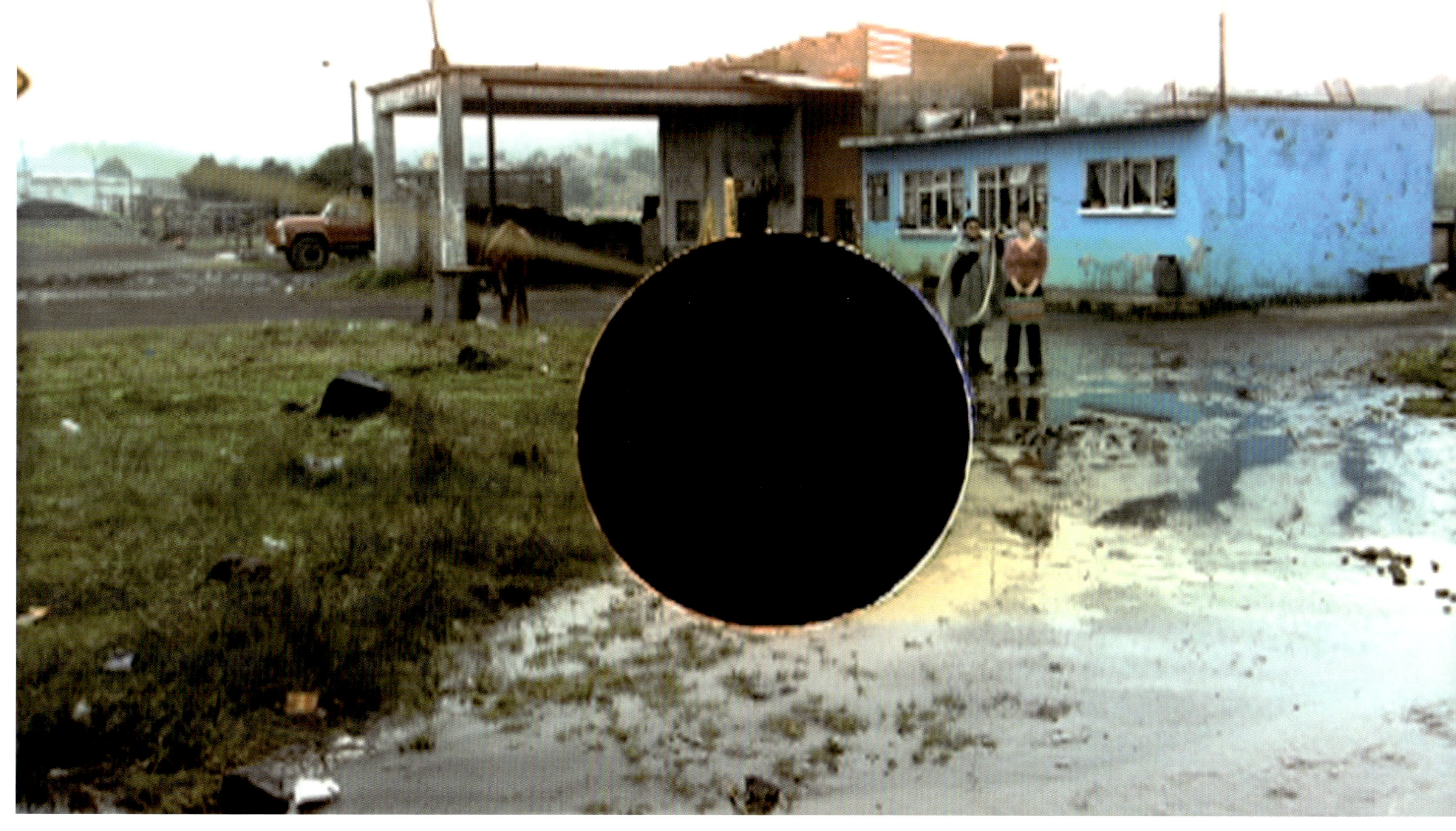

Stills from *Parres II*, 2004. 35mm transferred to DVD, 3 mins.

The eye scans over a mottled grey plane, its uneven texture indicating a hand-painted surface. Gradually the pigmentation begins to lose its fast, slipping and sliding into gestural swirls and smears, rivulets and drips; infinite variables of the original surface. A brief moment of creamy opacity, absolute neutrality, stills the image before the ground dissolves away to reveal the human agency at work beyond, a labourer washing a window framed by the scrubby landscape of a Mexican border town, an interloper upon the previously unattended surface. Wiping the last remnants of paint away, the labourer vanquishes the memory of the painting to reveal the 'real' world beyond.

The graduation from monochrome image to reality through this systematic action, from aesthetic non-place to corporeal present, occurs through a simultaneous process of erasure and disclosure. The two, it seems, cannot co-exist, one replaces the other, with the screen functioning as a Proscenium arch between them. What begins as a theatrical gesture, an abstract vocabulary of fluid mark-making, becomes locatable and rationalised in the world. The agency is revealed and a parallel drawn, perhaps, between artist and labourer, existing at opposite ends of the social spectrum yet whose productivity is rooted to the city. The landscape in Smith's work seems to reintroduce the idea of history painting, a desire to connect with time and place and to question the notion that a timeless and autonomous aestheticism could exist beyond the physical and social conditions of its making. It articulates the dialectic between art and production and the perpetual ricochet between them.

The breakdown of the picture surface is accompanied by a soundtrack of amplified sloshing sounds, a cartoon caricature of a cloth drenched in water, an exaggerated squeak of rag against glass, a performance of window cleaning in Technicolor. As the image dissolves into the landscape beyond these sounds mutate into barking dogs, a village band playing in the distance, romantically cinematic noises that seem fitting with the hazy, sun-baked scene. As the labourer, work complete, turns his back to the screen and walks away towards the town, the mechanical whirring of the camera dominates. This reality is also a construction.

Lizzie Carey-Thomas

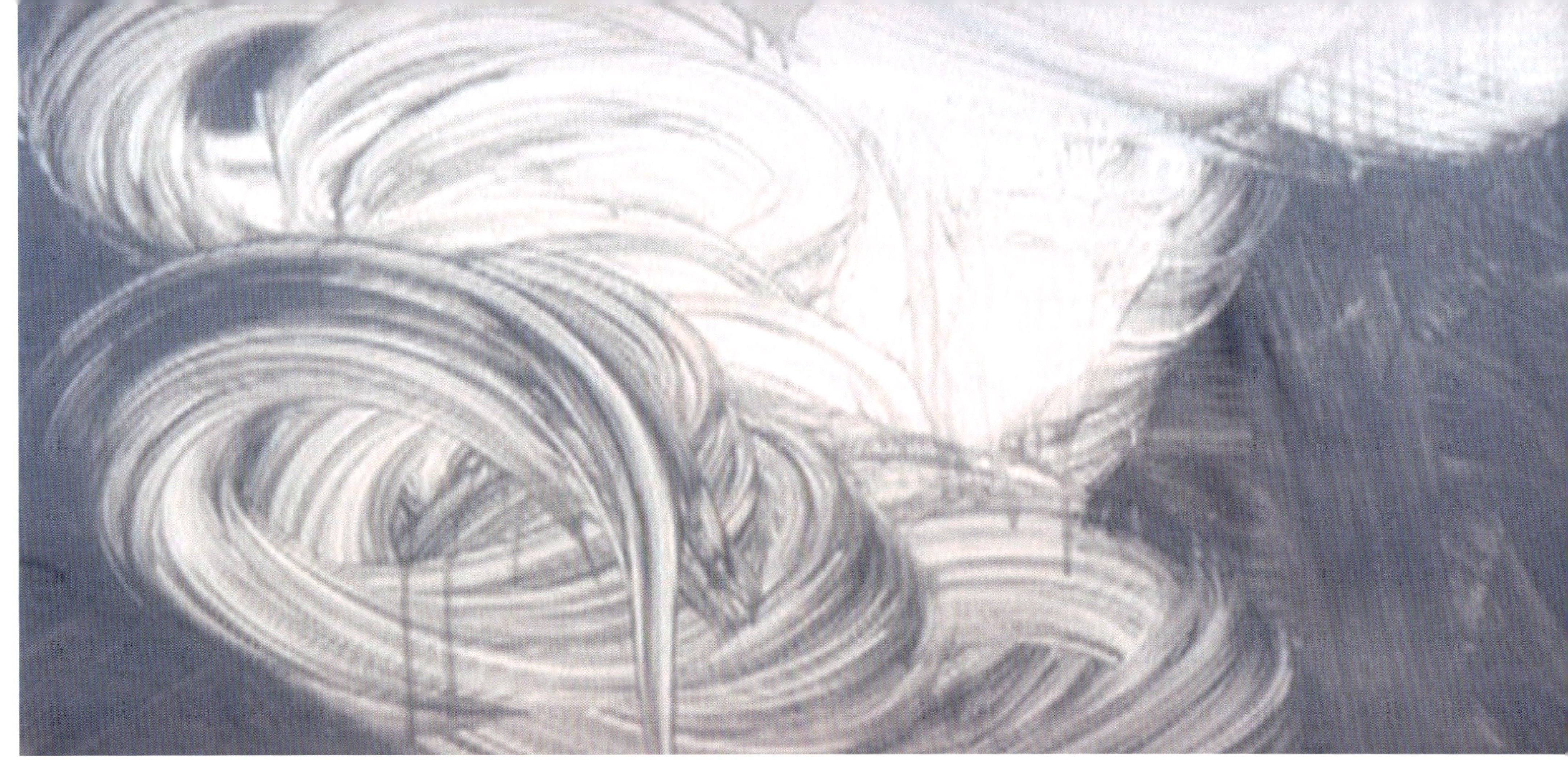

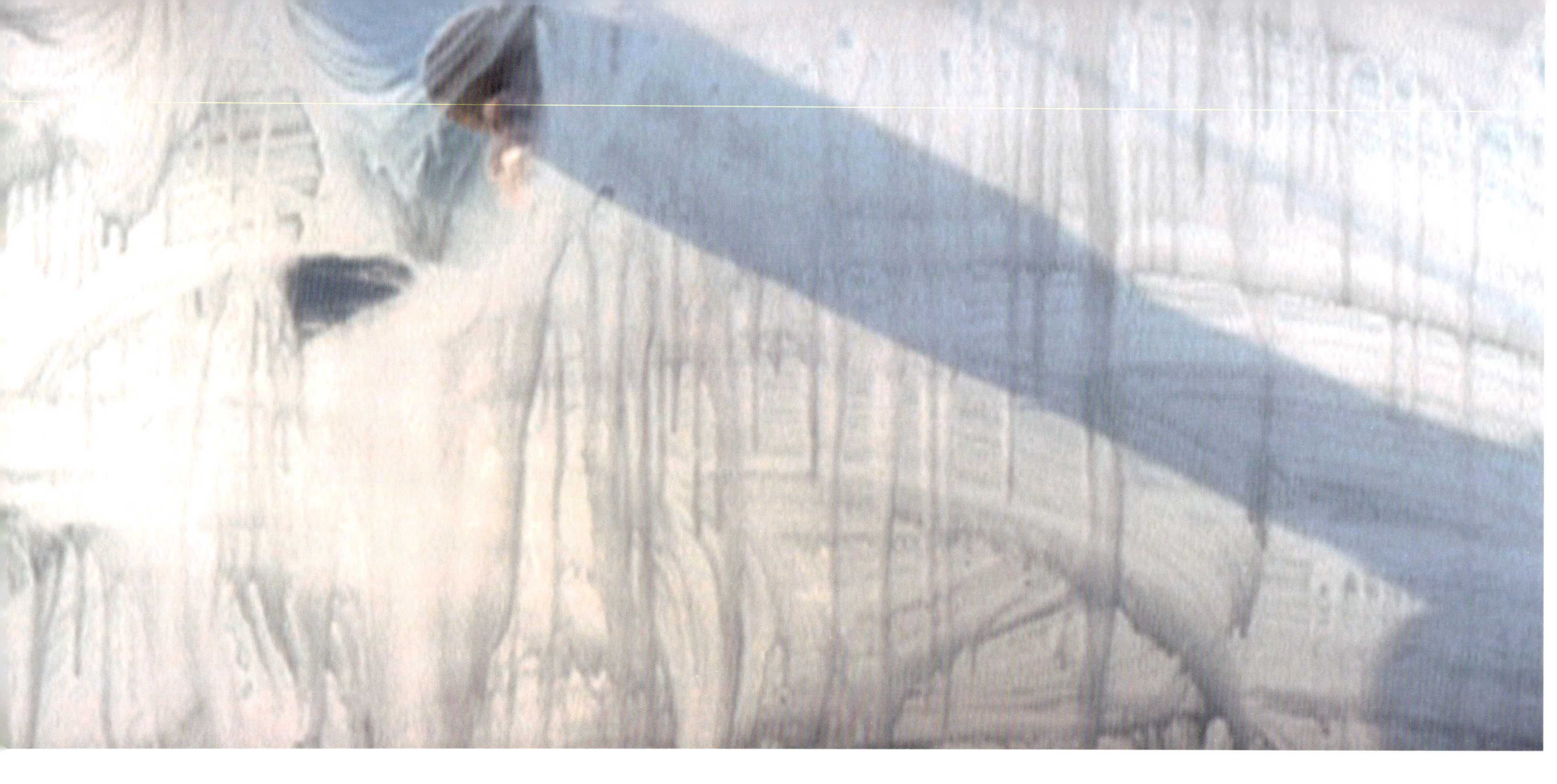

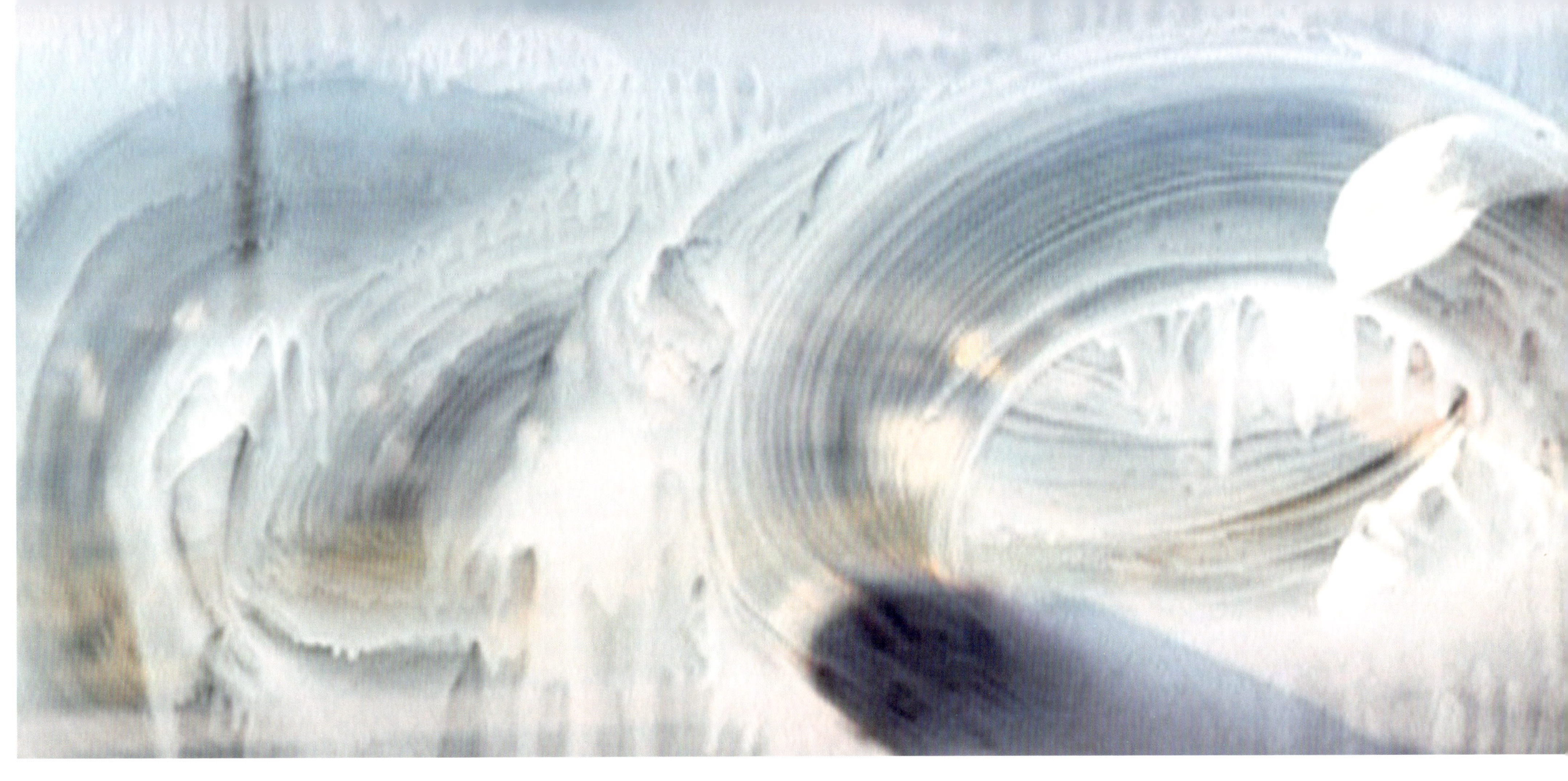

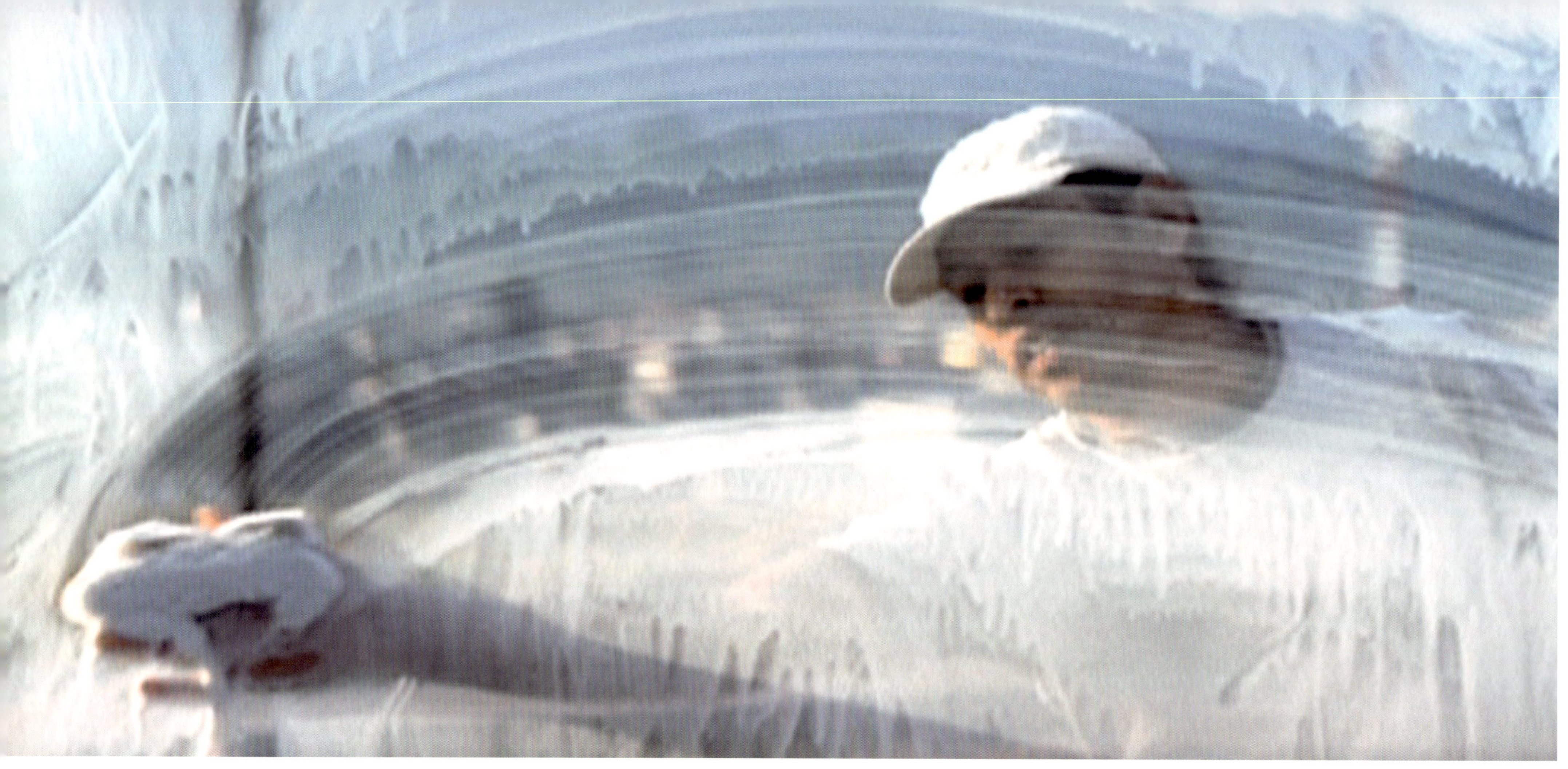

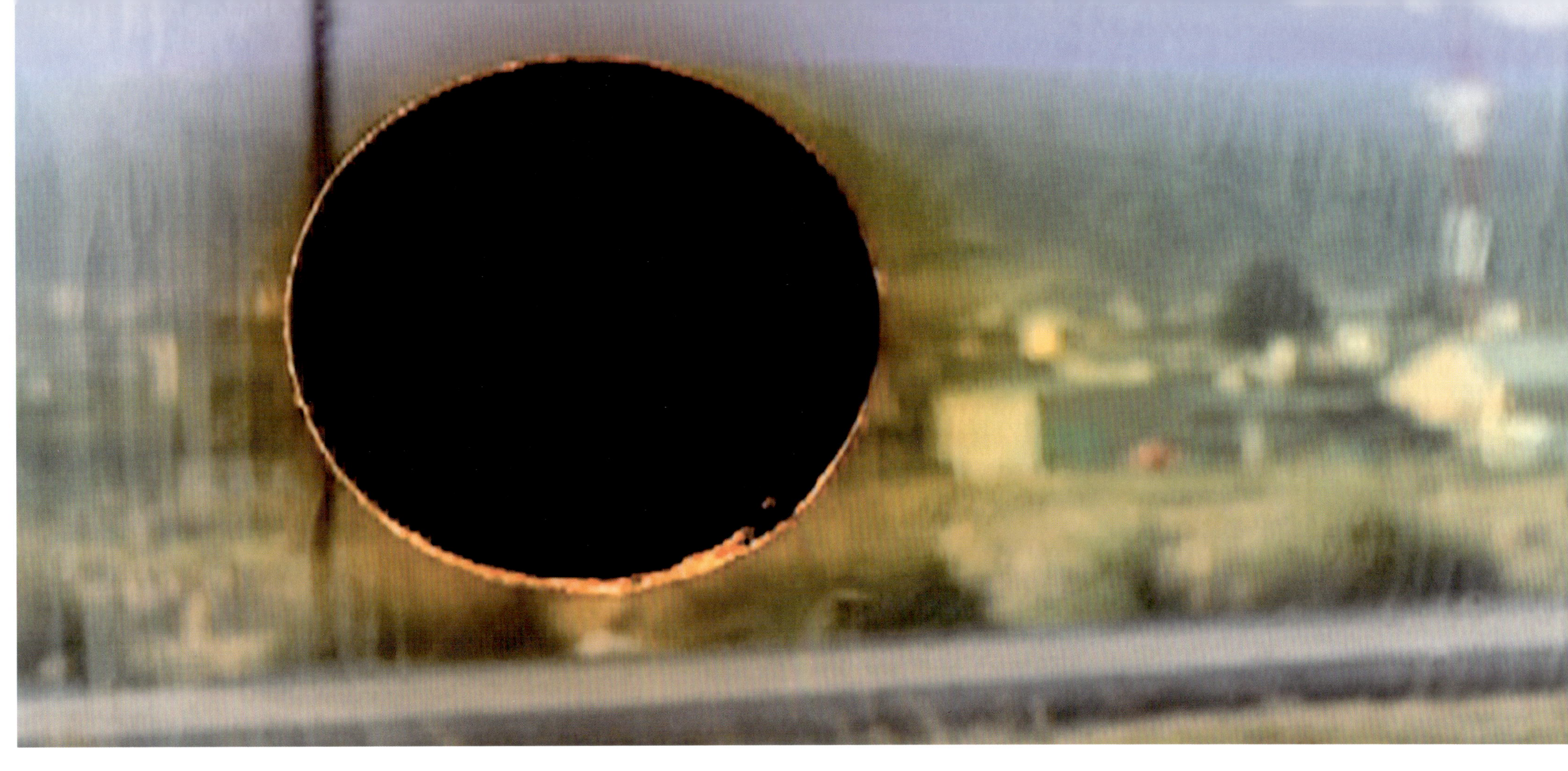

Stills from *Parres III*, 2005. 35mm transferred to DVD, 3 mins.

Walls

"I put up a picture on the wall. Then I forget there is a wall. I no longer know what there is behind this wall, and I no longer know there is a wall, I no longer know this wall is a wall, I no longer know what a wall is. I no longer know that in my apartment there are walls, and that if there weren't any walls, there would be no apartment. The wall is no longer what delimits and defines the space where I live, that which separates it from other places where other people live, it is nothing more than a support for the picture. But I also forget the picture, I no longer look at it, I know longer know how to look at it. I have put the picture on the wall so as to forget there was a wall, but in forgetting the wall I also forget the picture, too. There are pictures because there are walls. We have to be able to forget there are walls, and have found no better way to do that than pictures. Pictures efface walls. But walls kill pictures".

Georges Perec

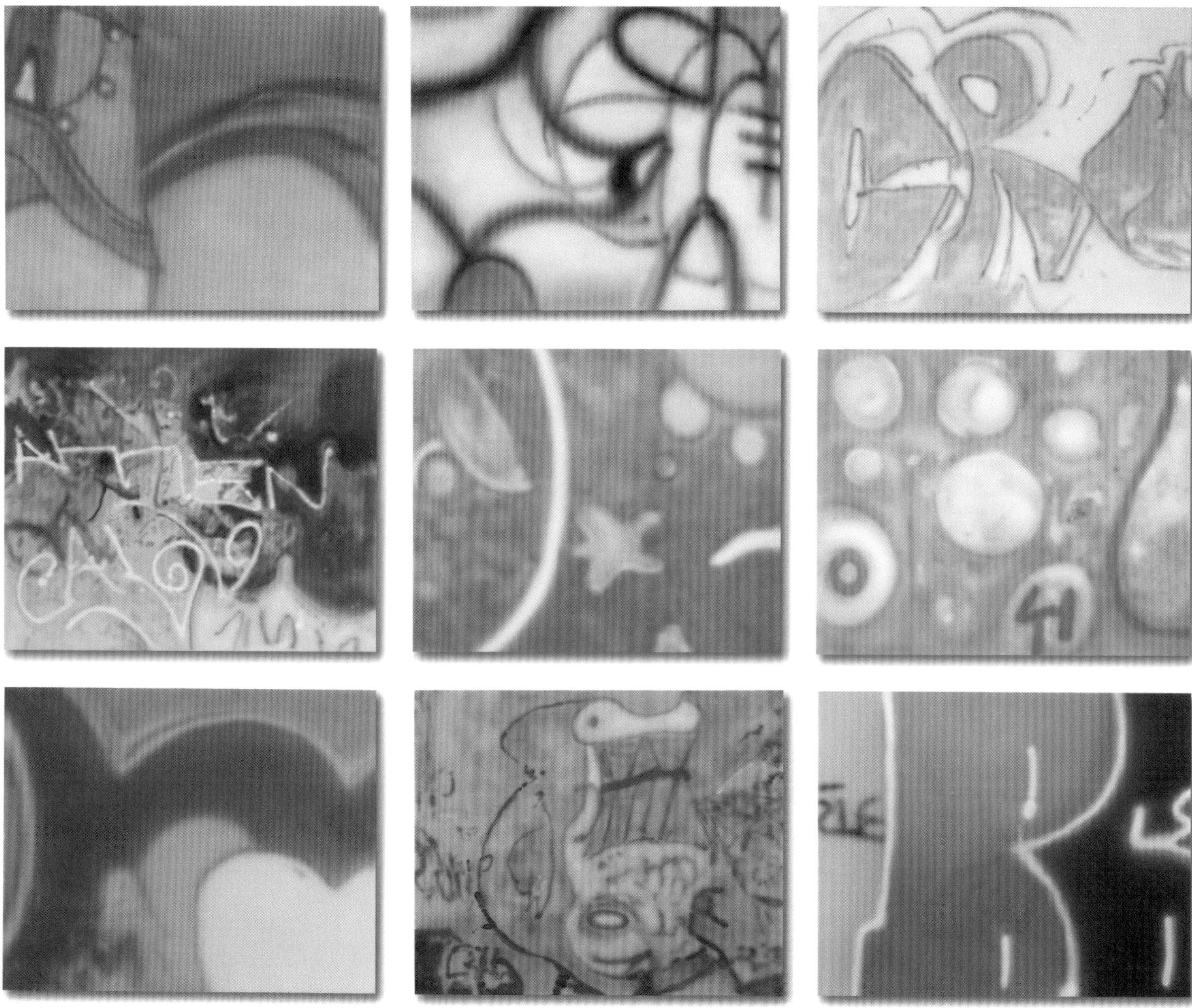

Nine graffiti paintings, 2006 – 7. Acrylic on MDF, 45 × 55 cm each

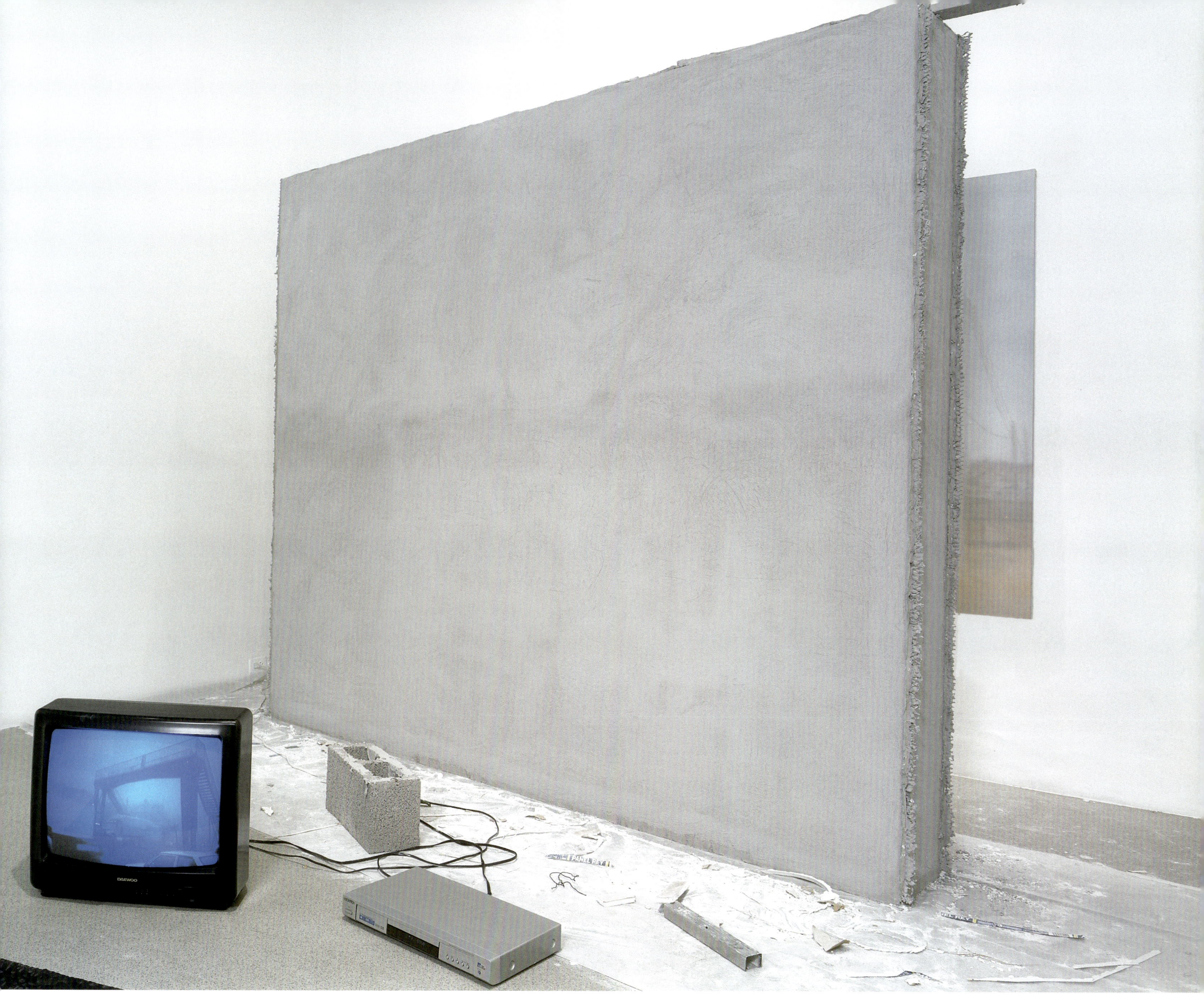

Installation for *Parres o*. Concrete and plywood wall. Painting 150 × 180 cm and video *Parres o* (Super 16 transferred to DVD)

List from notebook, 2006

10 Reasons to hide paintings. (behind walls).

1. To cut the illusion.
2. To replace the painting with another 'illusion'
3. To block your view.
4. View to what? → cut decoration.
5. ~~inside~~ because inside becomes outside.
6. Because _you_ don't want to 'see'. (what the eye doesn't see - the heart doesn't yearn for).
7. ~~Regla~~ Double window. - creates.
8. Limited vision of ~~spectator~~ viewer - squashes them. - presses them.
9. To question the experience of the gaze. (where does it come from geo-politically?).
10. Hide a 'bad' painting ~~too~~

Installation view of concrete wall, painting 45 × 55 cm and photograms from *Parres 0*

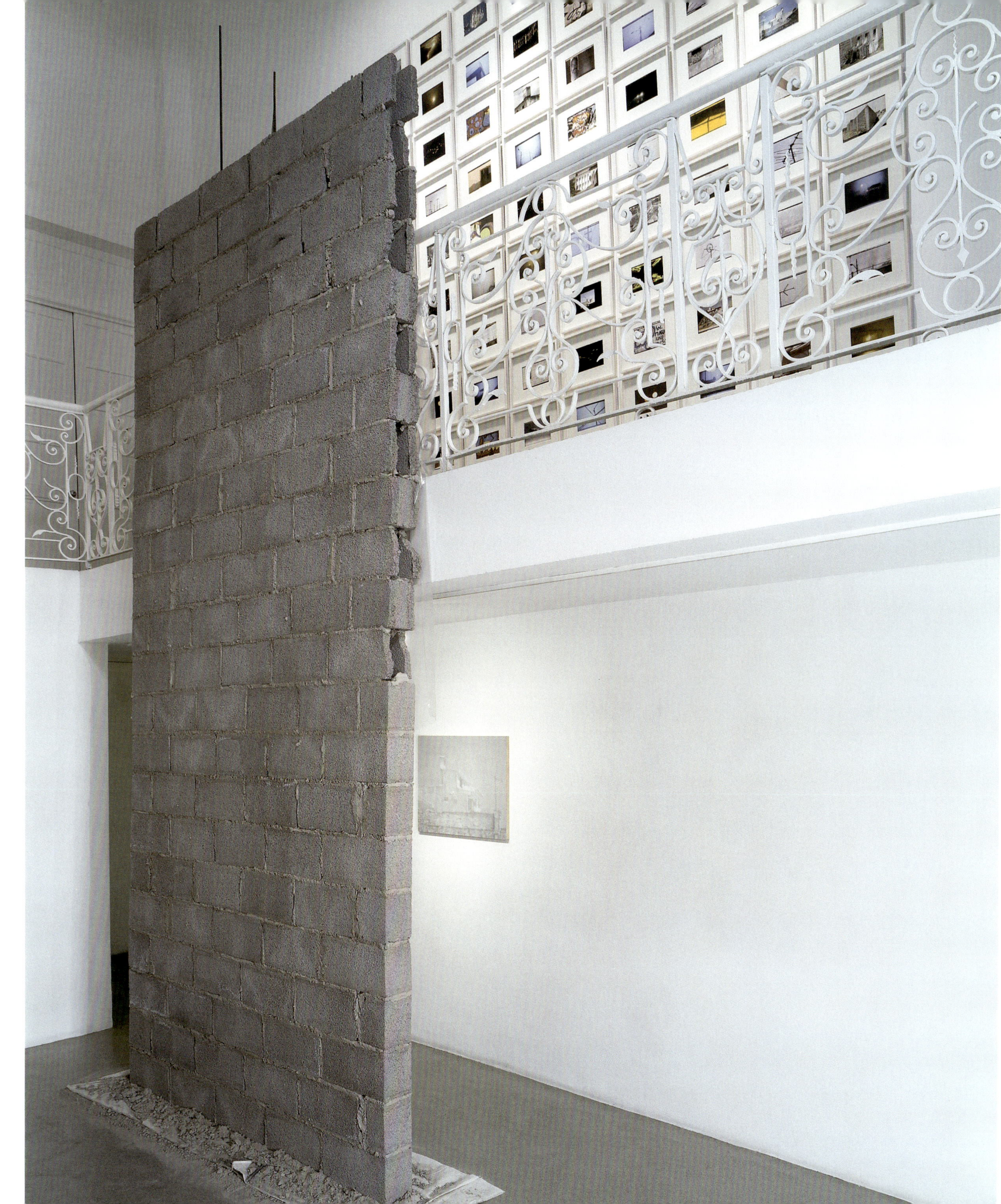

Monochrome. — Only see what there is.

Footnotes

Pages 24–26

1

The Spanish word *pueblo* can mean town or village, but also people, community, or nation. (Tr. note)

2

Referring to individuals who work for the police force and the army, but who also form part of the pueblo. (Tr. note)

Pages 48–54

1

Before studying the Nahuatl language group, Robert Hayward Barlow was personal secretary to Howard Phillips Lovecraft, the "Providence visionary" who created the Cthulhu mythos. He lived for years in Milpa Alta, one of the last areas where Náhuatl still remained relatively uninfluenced by Spanish. See R. H. Barlow, *The Extent of the Empire of the Culhua Mexica*, Berkeley & Los Angeles, University of California Press, 1949.

2

These brothels were gathering places for high-ranking politicians as well as for artists and writers; cf. Carlos Fuentes's *La región más transparente* (*Where the Air is Clear*) or Salvador Elizondo's *Farabeuf*.

3

This was not an isolated or innocuous phenomenon or undertaking: as of the 1950s, various "new settlements" were established in Mexico around schools or universities newly built on "virgin land" and were the starting point of important suburban agglomerations: only in Mexico City, the establish-ment of a campus of the Tecnológico de Monterrey in Coapa or of the Iberoamericana University in Santa Fe led to these areas' complete transformation, first drawing residents and then multinational business headquarters, eventually forming practically autonomous "neighborhoods."

4

For an analysis of Marín's imagery, see Dafne Cruz Porcini, "*Campesino sacrificado*" and "*Duelo por Zapata*" de Francisco Arturo Marín" in Renato González Mello et al., *La arqueología del régimen 1910–1955*, Museo Nacional de Arte, 2003, pp. 101–102.

5

Antonio Luna Arroyo, *Panorama de la escultura mexicana contemporánea*, Mexico City, INBA, 1964, p. 93.

6

In Rivera's eyes, the sculptures referenced Aztec imagery.

7

Diego Rivera, "Palabras a los que miren con los ojos de la sensibilidad y la inteligencia la obra de Marín" in Esther Acevedo (comp.), *Diego Rivera. Textos polémicos 2 (1950–1957)*, El Colegio Nacional, 1999, pp. 416–418.

8

I would like to thank Telly Duarte for her help and the precise details of *Campesino sacrificado*'s transportation and final placement.

9

Iván Gomezcésar Hernández, "Para que sepan los que aún no nacen… Construcción de la historia en Milpa Alta," Ph.D. dissertation, Universidad Autónoma Metropolitana, Unidad Iztapalapa, División de Ciencias Sociales y Humanidades, Departamento de Antropología, 2005; online: http://www.equidad.df.gob.mx/boletines/docs/ 2005_tesis_hist_milpa_alta.pdf

10

Mike Davis, *Planet of Slums*, London, Verso, 2006. This idea is not new: Fernand Braudel had already spoken of it in the late 1950s, and particularly in *Civilisation matérielle, économie et capitalisme: XVe-XVIIIe siècle*, Paris, Flammarion, 1979, referring to the increased speed of commercial goods transportation on land and sea, which left many trade centers (fairs or temporary markets) outside of the capitalist economic system. Davis adds an apocalyptic – and global – perspective to the issue, typical of the arch pessimistic vision of a nostalgic American left, and hence associated with "greens" and other idealistic environmental movements whose "solution" is to bemoan what has been lost rather than engage in precise actions.

Biography

1965
Born in Poole, UK.

Lives and works in Mexico City.

Selected individual exhibitions

2006–7
Spiral City and Other Vicarious Pleasures.
MUCA campus Mexico City, traveled to
The Lab. Denver, Colorado USA. Curated
by Cuauhtémoc Medina.

2007
Galeria OMR, Mexico City.

2006
Parres Trilogy, with Rafael Ortega.
Tate Britain, London Lightbox series.

2005
Galerie Peter Kilchmann, Zurich.

2004
Steps to Abstraction. In collaboration with
Rafael Ortega. San Diego Museum of
Contemporary Art. USA.

Selected group shows

2007
Global Cities. Tate Modern, London.

2006
What Makes You and I Different. Tramway,
Glasgow. Curated by Lorraine Wilson.

2005
New Acquisitions. MOMA, New York.
Curated by Klaus Biesenbach and Ann
Temkin.

2004
Sodium and Asphalt. Museum Tamayo,
Mexico City and Museum of Monterrey,
Monterrey, Mexico. Curated by Ann
Gallagher and Tobias Ostrander.

Thanks to:

Francis Alÿs, Paul Barker, Lutz Becker, Rina Carvajal, Alfonso Cornejo, Georgina Corrie, Olivier Debroise, Lizzie Carey-Thomas, Abraham Cruzvillegas, Pamela Echeverria, Giovanna Esposito Yussif, Alexandra Garcia Ponce, Maria Huesca, Virginie Kastel, Peter Kilchmann, Adam Lerner, Ana Belen Lezana, Yolanda Martinez, Patricia Ortiz Monasterio, Niki Nakazawa, Tobias Ostrander, Jaime Riestra, Francisco Rivera, Victor Sanchez, Fridolin Schonwiese, Guillermo Shelley, Carlos Walraven, Lorraine Wilson.

and always Rafael Ortega.

Parres was printed and bound in March 2008, at the workshops of EBS, Verona, Italy, on 150 grams Gardapat Kiara paper. Typeset in Fournier MT, made by Monotype in 1924 after designs by Pierre Simon Fournier circa 1742. The original print run is of 2000 copies. The supervision was done under the care of Herman Lelie.

Melanie Smith   Parres
Published by A&R Press/Turner

Edited by Melanie Smith
Design by Herman Lelie and Stefania Bonelli
Contributions by Melanie Smith, Francis Alÿs, Abraham Cruzvillegas, Tobias Ostrander, Olivier Debroise,
Rafael Ortega, Adam Lerner, Lorraine Wilson, Lizzie Carey-Thomas and Georges Perec

Translated from Spanish by Richard Moszka
Photography by Oliver Santana and Francisco Kochen
Proofreading by Debra Nagao
Color Separation by Emilio Breton

First edition, March 2008

Of this edition:
Compilation – including selection, placement and order of texts and images – copyright © 2007
Editorial G&P S.A. de C.V., unless otherwise noted, copyright © 2007 Melanie Smith
and the authors.

ISBN: 978-968-9056-34-8
Made in Mexico
Printed and bound in Italy

A&R Press/Turner books can be found in the
United Kingdom through:
ART DATA
12 Bell Industrial Estate
50 Cunnington Street
London W4 5HB
www.artdata.co.uk

A&R Press/Turner books can be found in Europe through:
Idea Books
Nieuwe Herengracht 11
Amsterdam 1011 RD
www.ideabooks.nl

A&R Press/Turner books can be found in the United States
and Canada through:
D.A.P/Distributed Art Publishers
155 Sixth Avenue
2nd Floor
New York, NY 10013
www.artbook.com

A&R Press/Turner books can be found in Mexico and Latin
America through:
Editorial Océano de México S.A. de C.V.
Blvd. Manuel Ávila Camacho No. 76, piso 10
Colonia Lomas de Chapultepec
Mexico City, 11000
www.oceano.com.mx

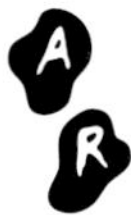

TURNER
Anatole France 13
Colonia Chapultepec Polanco
Mexico City, 15600
www.a-rpress.com
www.turnerlibros.com